Nick Vandome

Lightroom

In easy steps is an imprint of In Easy Steps Limited
16 Hamilton Terrace · Holly Walk · Leamington Spa
Warwickshire · United Kingdom · CV32 4LY
www.ineasysteps.com

In Easy Steps Limited supports The Forest Stewardship Council (FSC),
the leading international forest certification organization. All our titles
that are printed on Greenpeace approved FSC certified paper carry the
FSC logo.

Printed and bound in the United Kingdom

ISBN 978-1-78791-008-9

Contents

1 Introducing Lightroom

This chapter introduces
Lightroom – a versatile and
creative image-editing and
image-management app.
It shows how to install the
app, get to grips with the
interface, and see what's
happening in the Lightroom
community.

About Lightroom

Since its flagship product, Photoshop, was released in 1990, Adobe has been at the forefront of digital design and image editing and enhancement. This has included numerous different apps, enabling designers and home users to make the most of their creative talents using desktop computers, laptops, tablets, and smartphones to produce stunning photos and designs.

However, Adobe is well aware that the world of digital image editing and design is a fast-moving one, and it has moved with the times with all of its apps and services. The most important development in terms of the evolution of its products has been a significant move to provide online apps and services, in addition to making them available on traditional computing devices. This is done primarily through the online Creative Cloud subscription service, from which apps and additional options can be obtained. Once this has been done, apps can be used in a variety of ways:

- On computing devices such as desktop computers and laptops.

- On mobile devices such as tablets and smartphones, when connected to the internet.

- Via the web, to give access through a web browser.

A new range of apps has been developed by Adobe to make the most of the power and flexibility of Creative Cloud. For photographers, and anyone interested in editing digital images, Adobe Lightroom is one of the Creative Cloud apps that have helped to transform the way that people undertake much of their digital creativity.

Hot tip

Lightroom is an online, cloud-based subscription service. It can be downloaded from the Adobe website at **www. adobe.com**, for which an Adobe account and ID is required. This can be created, for free, with an email address and a password. Lightroom is part of the Creative Cloud suite of online apps, and an annual subscription is required to download it – see page 10 for details. Once it has been downloaded, images can be used in the online cloud and also on a local device, even if it is offline.

Don't forget

For more information about using Creative Cloud, see pages 14-17.

Lightroom anywhere

Not only does Lightroom have powerful image-editing features, but it also operates in the cloud so that images are saved here and can be accessed from a range of devices and locations, provided that there is an internet connection. There are versions for mobile devices, and also a web version so that you can access Lightroom and all of your images there from a web browser.

Hot tip

If you are signed in with the same Adobe account, the images that you see in all versions of Lightroom will be the same. Any edits or additions made in one version will automatically then be available in the other versions too.

Mobile version of Lightroom for smartphones and tablets

Don't forget

For more information about using the mobile version of Lightroom, see Chapter 8.

Web version of Lightroom, viewed through a browser

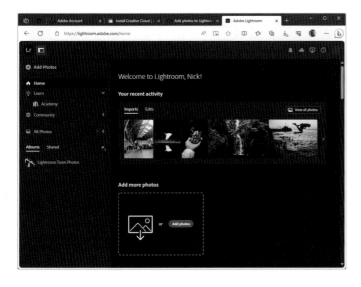

Don't forget

For more information about using Lightroom on the web, see Chapter 9.

Obtaining Lightroom

Lightroom can be obtained and downloaded from the Adobe website at **www.adobe.com**

It requires an annual subscription, and there is a free 7-day trial for the app. It can be downloaded individually or as part of a plan that includes additional apps. To obtain Lightroom:

Hot tip

If the option in Step 1 is not available on the homepage, click on the **Creativity & Design** option on the top toolbar and select Lightroom in the **Featured products** section.

Don't forget

Price plans can be for individual Creative Cloud apps (e.g. Lightroom); a Photography plan; or a plan containing all of the Creative Cloud apps. All price plans have a 7-day free trial period, after which there is an annual subscription, paid either monthly or annually. Card details for payment are taken at the start of the free trial, but if this is canceled before the end of the 7-day period, there is no charge.

1 Access the Adobe website at **www.adobe.com** Scroll down the homepage and click on the **Learn more** option in the **Adobe Photoshop Lightroom** panel

2 Click on the **Free trial** button

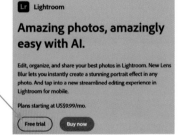

3 Select the required plan for Lightroom (see the Don't Forget tip) and click on the **Continue** button

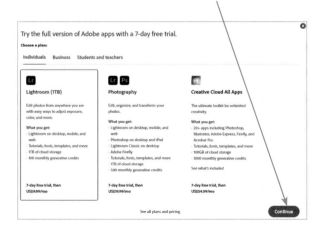

4 Confirm the plan for Lightroom and click on the **Continue** button

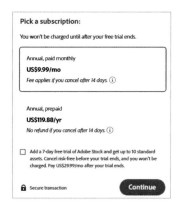

5 If required, additional items can be added to an individual plan for Lightroom. The **Summary** box displays items that have been selected. Once this has been checked, click on the **Continue** button

6 Enter your email address, which will be used to set up an Adobe account ID, with a password. Click on the **Continue** button to set up your Adobe ID, then complete payment details and download the Lightroom installation app – see pages 12-13

If you initially only want to use Lightroom, additional apps can be added at a later date from the Creative Cloud app – see page 15 for details about this.

Once you have created an Adobe ID, this can be used to access all versions of Lightroom (desktop, mobile and web) using the same sign-in details (email and password).

Since the subscription for Creative Cloud apps is on an annual basis, make sure that you definitely want to use an app before you obtain it.

Installing Lightroom

Once the steps on pages 10-11 have been completed, the set-up file for Lightroom will have been downloaded to the Downloads section of your browser or to your Downloads folder. This can be used to start the installation process.

The interface for the Windows and Mac versions of Lightroom is identical. The only differences are with standard keyboard controls – e.g. right-click in Windows and **Ctrl** + click in Mac. The Mac version can be installed from the set-up file in the Downloads folder.

1 Double-click on the **Lightroom_Set-Up.exe** file in your Downloads folder. This will then run automatically and install relevant items

Lightroom_Set-Up.exe
2.9 MB — adobe.com — October 11

2 The set-up file will install the Creative Cloud Desktop, which is a dashboard for managing all of the apps and services within Creative Cloud, including Lightroom. Click on the **All apps** option in the left-hand sidebar

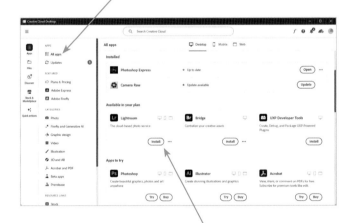

Creative Cloud can be opened at any time by clicking on this button from the Start menu in Windows or the Launchpad in macOS:

Adobe Creative Cloud
New

3 All available apps are displayed in the main panel. Click on the **Install** button for **Lightroom**

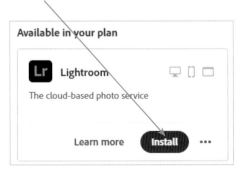

4 Click on the **Desktop** tab to have this version of Lightroom installed, and ensure that there is a white checkmark in a green circle next to **Works on this device**

5 Click on the **Install** button

6 During the installation process there will be an option to download some sample photos, which can be useful when getting started with Lightroom. Click on the **Start now** button

7 Lightroom will be opened, with sample photos displayed, in the **All Photos** section

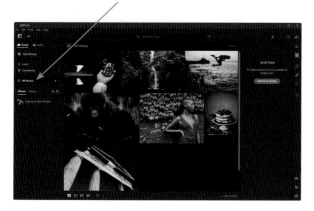

Don't forget

If Lightroom does not open at the end of the installation process, click on this button from the Start menu in Windows or the Launchpad in macOS:

Don't forget

Lightroom is designed as an online cloud-based service, with images in the cloud being stored and backed up on Adobe's own computers (servers). Cloud view is the default view in Lightroom. However, there is also Local view (desktop version) or Device view (mobile version) that can be used to view and edit images that are only stored on your device and not in the cloud. Local images can easily be moved into the Cloud section so that they are available on all of your devices.

13

About Creative Cloud

Creative Cloud is essentially an online service for accessing apps and content from Adobe. However, it also has its own app interface that is downloaded at the same time as any of the Creative Cloud apps that you want to use – in this case, Lightroom. The Creative Cloud app serves as a dashboard for accessing all of its related apps and services.

The apps within Creative Cloud are available through a subscription service, either individually or as a bundle of several apps, known as plans.

When an app from the Creative Cloud suite is downloaded, the Creative Cloud app is also downloaded. This then becomes available with the rest of the apps on your device. There are numerous functions and features within the Creative Cloud app that help to enhance your online experience with Lightroom and any other apps that you want to use.

1 Access and open the Creative Cloud app in the same way as with any other app on your device

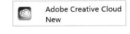

2 Click on the **Desktop** tab at the top of the window to view available items for your device. Use the toolbar and sidebar to navigate around the Creative Cloud app

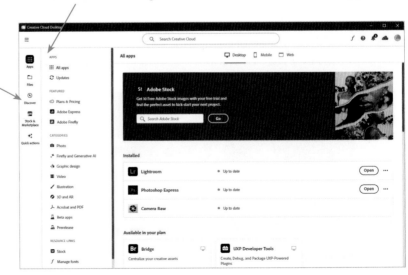

Don't forget

The toolbar at the left-hand side of the sidebar contains options for **Apps**; **Files**; **Discover**; **Stock & Marketplace**; and **Quick actions**. For each one, additional options are available to the right of the toolbar in the sidebar.

14

3 Click on the **All apps** button in the sidebar to view installed and available apps

4 Any installed apps are displayed in the **Installed** section

If there are updates for installed Creative Cloud apps, these will be displayed in Step 4. Click on an update to keep your apps as up-to-date as possible. Click on the **Open** button in Step 4 to open a Creative Cloud app from here.

5 The **Available in your plan** section contains apps that are automatically included in your current subscription plan at no additional cost. Click on the **Install** button to download these apps, as required

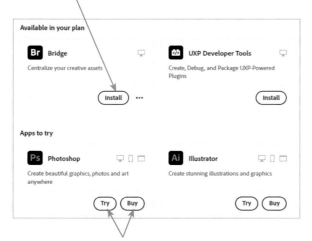

If you use Creative Cloud apps other than those in the **Available in your plan** section, there will be an additional subscription charge.

6 The **Apps to try** section contains a range of apps that are relevant to any that you have already obtained – e.g. Lightroom. Click on the **Try** button next to an app to download a free trial, or click on the **Buy** button to purchase it

...cont'd

7 In the **Apps** section, click on one of the items under the **Categories** heading in the sidebar to view the relevant range of apps according to the selected category. Click on each item to view more details about it

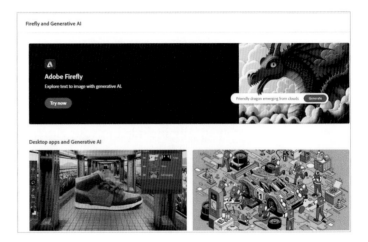

The online tutorials and live streaming events require an internet connection.

8 Click on the **Discover** button in the sidebar to view online tutorials and live streaming events about getting the best out of the Creative Cloud apps, including Lightroom

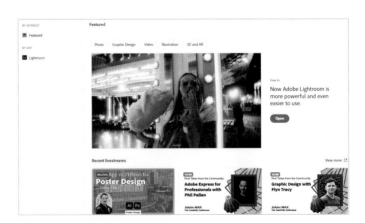

9   Click on the **Stock & Marketplace** button in the sidebar to access a huge range of stock photos and videos that can be used with the Creative Cloud apps for digital projects

Stock & Marketplace

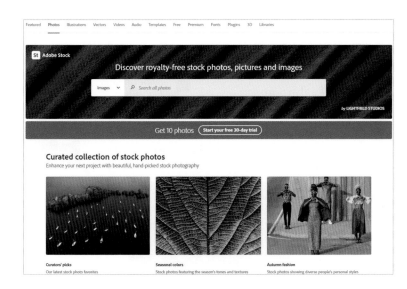

Beware

An additional subscription is required for one of the plans for using the stock Adobe images in Step 9.

10   Click on the **Quick actions** button in the sidebar to perform a range of quick wins on your photos using the functionality of the Adobe Express app (see the Don't forget tip). Click on an item to add your own photos and have an action performed on it

Quick actions

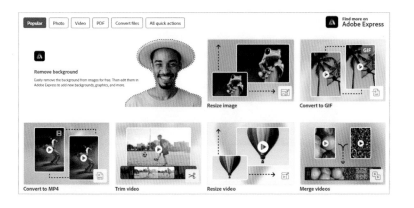

Don't forget

Adobe Express is a free stand-alone app that is used for creative designs for images and videos. It can be downloaded using the Creative Cloud app, from the Adobe website, or from online app stores, including Apple's App Store, Google Play, and Microsoft Store. In the example in Step 10, images can be uploaded to utilize specific functions of Adobe Express, although this is not done with the app itself. The basic version is free, and you can also upgrade to the paid-for Premium version.

Starting with Lightroom

Desktop Cloud view

The desktop version of Lightroom has two areas where you can work with your digital images: Cloud view and Local view. Cloud view is where images are stored online, and Local view is the contents of your desktop or laptop computer. To get started with Cloud view:

1 Click on this button to open Lightroom

2 Click on the **Cloud** tab at the top of the window to view the available items

Click on the **All Photos** option in Step 2 to display all photos in Cloud view in the main window. Click on the **Add Photos** button to import photos from your desktop or laptop computer (Local view – see the next page).

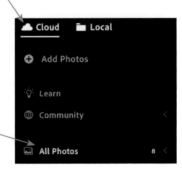

3 Images that are in the Cloud section of Lightroom are displayed in the main window

4 Click on these buttons to change the viewing options

...cont'd

Desktop Local view
To get started with Lightroom Local view:

1 Click on the **Local** tab at the top of the window

2 Click on the **Browse** tab in the left-hand sidebar to navigate through the folders on your desktop or laptop

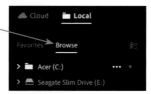

19

Hot tip

Images from Local view can easily be copied over to Cloud view, and it is best to do this so that they can be accessed on multiple devices, and also because they are backed up in Cloud view. To do this, select an image in Step 3 and click on the **Copy [] Photo to Cloud** option.

3 Click on the **Favorites** tab to view any folders that have been marked as favorites. The **Pictures** folder, and its sub-folders, is included as a favorite by default.
Click on a folder to view its content in the main window

Lightroom Interface

Although Local view and Cloud view both operate slightly differently in Lightroom, the general interface is the same. To get started with the interface:

Sidebar
Click on this button in the top left-hand corner of the Lightroom window to show or hide the left-hand sidebar.

Don't forget

If the sidebar is hidden, this ensures more room in the main window for viewing images.

Menu bar
Click on the options on the top menu bar to view selected items.

Edit menu

Photo menu

File menu

View menu

Help menu

Don't forget

For more details about using the Help menu, see page 30.

20

Grids

Photos in Lightroom can be displayed in a variety of formats. Click on these buttons at the bottom of the Lightroom window to view the different grid options, from left to right:

Photo Grid

Beware

The Photo Grid option is not available in Local view.

Hot tip

Drag on this slider in the bottom right-hand corner of the main window to zoom in or zoom out on images in the main window:

Square Grid

21

...cont'd

Compare

Don't forget

Click on one of the images in Compare view to make it the active one. Editing changes can then be applied to it without affecting the other image.

Detail

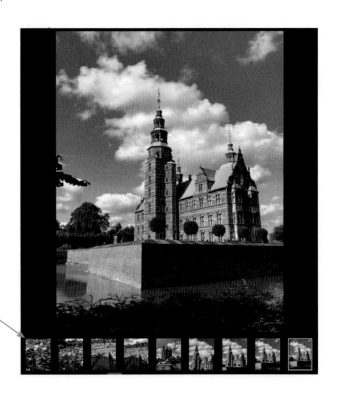

Hot tip

In both Compare and Detail view, the Filmstrip is available at the bottom of the window. Scroll left or right to view all available images and click on one to view it in the main window.

Editing options

In Compare view and Detail view, the editing tools are available at the right-hand side of the window.

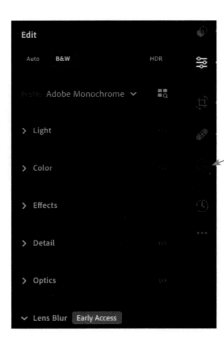

Click on these buttons at the right-hand side of the editing panel to access more editing options and categories.

Click on an arrowhead next to one of the editing categories to expand it and access the full range of options for the category.

For a detailed look at the editing functions in the desktop version of Lightroom, see Chapter 6.

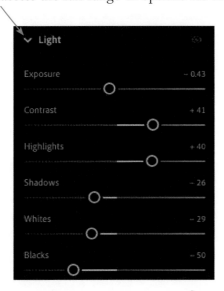

Lightroom Community

When using Lightroom, you are not alone. There is a whole community of other Lightroom users who share work that they have done with the app and make editing options available to the wider Lightroom community. These edits can be saved as presets, and you can also add your own edits to ones that other people have created. To use Lightroom Community:

Don't forget

For a detailed look at presets in the desktop version of Lightroom, see Chapter 4. For a detailed look at editing images in the desktop version of Lightroom, see Chapters 6 and 7.

 1 In Cloud view, click on the **Community** option to access it in the main window

2 Click on the left-pointing arrowhead next to the **Community** heading to expand its options in the sidebar

3 In the main window, the Community options are displayed at the top of the window

Hot tip

When you open an image from a Lightroom Community member, you can see the original image, any edits that have been applied to it, and the final image.

4 Click on the **For You** option on the top toolbar to view recommended image edits from Community members

5 Move the cursor over an image to view the available options. These can include **Remix** and **Save as Preset**

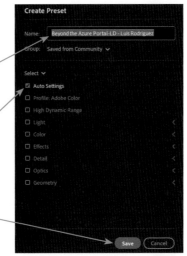

The options in Step 5 are determined by the settings applied by the individual Community member. In some instances, the **Remix** option will not be available.

6 For the **Save as Preset** option in the previous step, keep the original name for the edited image or enter your own name for it

7 Check **On** the checkboxes for elements of the edited image that you want to keep, then click on the **Save** button to save the preset version

8 For the **Remix** option in Step 5, perform editing changes on the image as required, then click on the **Next** button

If an image in Lightroom Community has this icon below it, it means that the image can be remixed:

If there is a number next to the icon, this indicates how many remixes have been performed on the image.

9 Enter a comment about your remix as required, then click on the **Post Remix** button to post your edited image to Lightroom Community so that other members can view it and edit it too

...cont'd

Saving to Lightroom Community
To save your own edited images to Lightroom Community:

Beware

If an image has had minimal editing applied to it – for instance, only one or two editing steps – then you will not be able to share it with Lightroom Community.

Hot tip

Images can also be shared with Lightroom Community by selecting them in any view, clicking on the  **Share** button on the top toolbar, and clicking on the **Share to Community...** option.

Images can also be shared by right-clicking on them (Windows) or **Ctrl** + clicking on them (Mac) and selecting **Share to Community...**.

1 Click on the **Recent Edits** option in the Lightroom sidebar

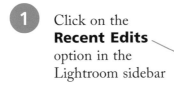

2 Click on an image in **Photo Grid** view or **Square Grid** view to select it (only images to which editing has been applied will be displayed in this window). Click on the **Share to Community** button

3 Enter a title for the shared image and an optional description of your editing process

4 Select at least one category for the image, to help people in Lightroom Community search for it

5 Drag the **Enable 'Save as Preset'** and **Allow Remixing** buttons **On** or **Off** as required, to enable or prevent these particular permissions for other Community users viewing your image

...cont'd

Following people in Lightroom Community

Within the Community section it is possible to follow other users – in a similar way to following people on social media sites – so that you can quickly see their latest published edited images. To follow someone in Lightroom Community:

1 Click on the **Following** tab on the top toolbar

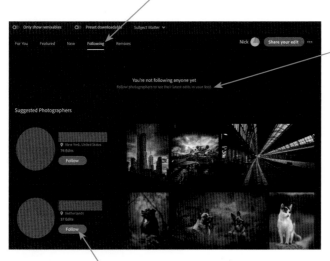

Once you have followed someone, their details appear at the top of the **Following** panel, where you will be able to view their edits and be notified about new ones that are added.

2 Click on the **Follow** button next to a person you want to follow

3 Click on the **Follow** button in the next window to confirm the action

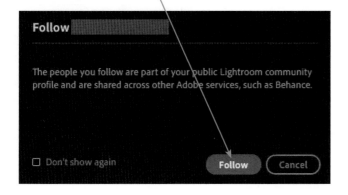

Check **On** the **Don't show again** checkbox in Step 3 to avoid this window being displayed each time you follow someone:

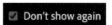

Exporting Images

Lightroom does not have a traditional Save function, as all editing changes are automatically saved as new versions of the image, with the original remaining intact. However, images (either originals or edited versions) can be exported into different file formats or the same format but with different settings. To do this:

1 Select an image to be exported. This can be in any of the Lightroom views

Don't forget

The other options in the Share panel are for **Share**, which can be used to share images with family and friends (see pages 185-186), and sharing with **Lightroom Community** (see pages 24-27).

2 Click on the **Share** button on the top toolbar

3 The **Export** options are displayed at the top of the Share panel. Click on the **Custom Settings...** option to specify your own settings for the exported image (see the next page)

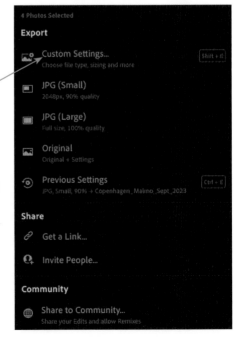

4 Click on one of the other export options – e.g. **JPG (Large)** – to export the image into this format

5 For the **Custom Settings...** option in Step 3 on the previous page, the image is displayed in the main window, with the settings in the right-hand panel

6 Select settings for the exported image as required. These include **Image Type**, **Dimensions**, and **Quality**; options for metadata to be copied with the image; and **File Naming** options

7 Click on the **Export [ ] Photo** button to export the image

8 For all of the export options, File Explorer (Windows) or Finder (Mac) are automatically opened. Navigate to the required folder to save the image

Don't forget

By default, the selected folder for exporting images in Step 8 is **Lightroom Saved Photos**, which is a folder that is created automatically when Lightroom is installed. However, any other folder can also be selected as the destination location for exported images.

Help Options

Lightroom has several useful options for finding out more about the app and how to get the most out of it. To access and use some of these options:

1 Access the **Help** menu, as shown on page 20

Lightroom Help

There is also a **Lightroom Help** option:

Items on the Help menu include options for starting the process to obtain Lightroom on mobile devices and on the web.

> Get Lightroom on mobile...
> Lightroom for web...

1 The **Lightroom Help** option is an online help service that opens in your device's default browser

Other items on the Help menu include options for managing your Adobe account and also accessing any updates that are available for Lightroom.

> Manage My Account...
> Sign Out... (NICKVANDOME@MAC.COM)
> Updates...

2 Click on one of the options above – e.g. **User Guide** – to view the full range of options. Click on individual categories to expand them and view their contents

Adobe Lightroom User Guide

> Introduction
> In-app learning
> Add, import, and capture photos
> Organize photos
> Edit photos
> Edit videos
> Save, share, and export
> Lightroom for mobile, TV, and the web
> Migrate photos

Guided Tutorials

This option can be used for step-by-step tutorials for specific image-editing techniques.

1 Click on one of the options in the Guided Tutorials window – e.g. **Perfect an Outdoor Portrait**

2 Click on the **Start Tutorial** button

As a guided tutorial progresses, there are prompts to select the required item for each step so that you can perform all necessary tasks in the process.

3 The tutorial identifies any issues with the image and shows how to correct them. Click on the **Continue** button to progress through the tutorial

...cont'd

Online Tutorials

The **Online Tutorials** option provides similar online help options to Lightroom Help on page 30.

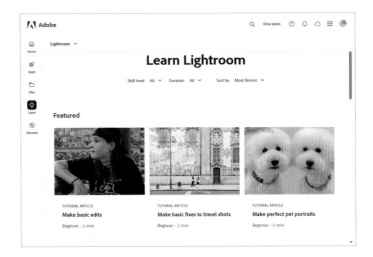

Getting Started with Lightroom

For the **Getting Started with Lightroom** option, click on this button at the right-hand side of the top toolbar in the main window: It contains several options:

Hot tip

If a photo is being viewed in Detail view, there will be a **Learn with my photo** option at the top of the **Getting Started with Lightroom** panel. Click on the **Edit Your Photo** option to view a guided tutorial that will edit your own image.

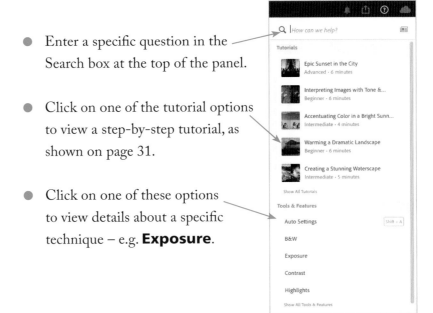

- Enter a specific question in the Search box at the top of the panel.

- Click on one of the tutorial options to view a step-by-step tutorial, as shown on page 31.

- Click on one of these options to view details about a specific technique – e.g. **Exposure**.

2 Local and Cloud Lightroom

One of the great strengths of Lightroom is that images can be stored in the cloud and then accessed on a variety of devices. This chapter shows how to do this, and also how to work with Local view.

Starting with Local View

There are two options for viewing and editing images in the desktop version of Lightroom: Local view and Cloud view. Local view can be used to access all of the images on your computer, from where you can manage and edit them. It is also possible to add them to Cloud view from Local view.

The overall interface of Local view and Cloud view is similar.

The main difference between the two views is the sidebar, which offers separate functionality.

Local view
(Browse and Favorites)

Cloud view

Hot tip

Folders and files can be browsed and accessed in Local view without the need to have an internet connection, unlike Cloud view.

Browse in Local View

The Browse option in Local view provides access to the contents of your desktop or laptop computer, and you can navigate around it in a similar way to using File Explorer (Windows) or Finder (Mac). This can be the starting point for accessing folders and images so that they can be used within Lightroom. To do this:

1 Click on the **Local** tab on the top toolbar and click on the **Browse** tab

2 Your computer's hard drive and any connected external drives are displayed

3 Click on a right-pointing arrowhead to expand an item

The folder structure in the Browse section mirrors the same structure on your computer – this is where it is taken from by Lightroom.

4 Keeping expanding folders until you can see the one that you want to access (e.g. the **Users** folder) and then navigate to your own user folder

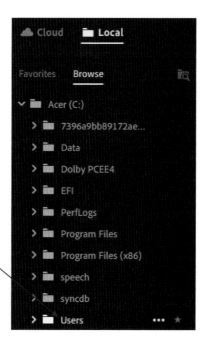

...cont'd

5 If a folder does not contain any images, this will be indicated in the main window. For instance, the main **Users** folder may not contain any specific images

6 Expand a folder that contains images – e.g. the **Pictures** folder

7 Click on a folder to view its contents in the main window

8 The images in the folder are displayed in different formats, depending on the view that has been selected

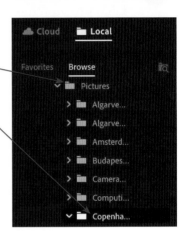

Don't forget

Click on these buttons at the bottom of the window to select the required view options:

In Local view, these are Square Grid, Compare, and Detail.

Favorites in Local View

The Favorites tab in Local view can be used to assign specific folders so that you can quickly access all of your favorite images. To do this:

1 Click on the **Favorites** tab in Local view. By default, it contains your computer's **Pictures** folder

2 To add a folder to the Favorites tab, click on the **Local** tab and navigate to the required folder

3 Move the cursor over the required folder to display menu options, to the right of the folder name

Hot tip

Folders can also be added as favorites by clicking on the star icon next to the folder name so that it becomes solid.

4 Click on the **Add as Favorite** option

> Add as Favorite
> Copy to Cloud
>
> Rename Folder...
> Create Folder in "Copenhagen_Malmo_Sept_2023"
>
> Show in Explorer

5 Click on the **Favorites** tab to view the newly added folder. Folders are displayed in alphabetic order. Click on the folder to view its images in the main window

Hot tip

To remove a folder from the Favorites list, move the cursor over it to access the menu as in Step 3, and click on the **Remove from Favorites** option. Or, click on the star icon so that it is not solid.

37

Local Folder Menu Options

In Local view, the Browse section contains a menu for folders that are being viewed. This can be used to manage and customize folders. To do this:

1 Access the menu for a folder, as shown in Step 3 on page 37

Don't forget

If items are added to Cloud view, they are not removed from Local view.

2 Click on the **Copy to Cloud** option to copy the selected folder to the Cloud view of Lightroom

3 Click on the **Rename Folder...** option to change the name of the folder. Overtype with a new name, as required

4 Click on the **Create Folder in [folder name]** option to create a sub-folder. Enter a name for the sub-folder

Don't forget

If a sub-folder is created within a main one, this is also included within the folder structure on your computer, not just within Lightroom. This is also the case if a folder is renamed.

5 Click on the **Create** button to add the sub-folder within the original one

From Local to Cloud

Being able to transfer images from Local view to Cloud view is an important feature of Lightroom so that images can then be accessed and edited through a mobile device and also through a web browser, providing maximum flexibility. One option is to use the **Copy to Cloud** option in Step 2 on the previous page to copy a complete folder of images. It is also possible to copy individual images.

① In **Square Grid** view, click on a single image to select it, or select the first image and press **Shift** + click to select a sequential group of images

Press **Ctrl** + click (Windows) or **Command** + click (Mac) to select a non-sequential group of images.

② Click on the **Copy [ ] Photos to Cloud** button in the top right-hand corner of the window

③ Review the details about copying the image(s) and click on the **OK** button

Individual images can also be copied to Cloud view from the **Compare** and **Detail** options in Local view by clicking on a single image and clicking on the button in Step 2.

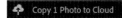

④ Click on the **Cloud** tab to view the copied image(s), which appear at the top of the window

Opening Images in Local View

In addition to being able to access images on your own computer, Local view also has a feature whereby you can open images from external devices, such as a flashdrive, so that you can view and edit a wider range of images. To do this:

1 In the **Browse** section of Local view, click on this icon

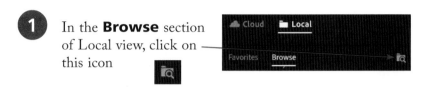

2 Navigate to a folder that you want to open in Local view – e.g. a folder on a flashdrive

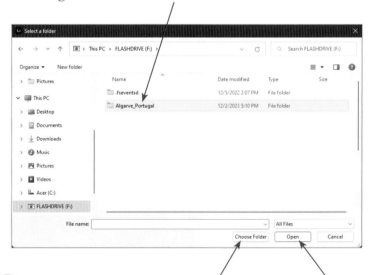

Don't forget

Any external device containing images connected to your computer can be accessed via Lightroom, and the images can be opened as required.

3 Click on the **Choose Folder** button to use the whole folder, or click on the **Open** button to open the folder and select individual images within it

4 The folder is added to the **Browse** section in the Local view sidebar (even if only an individual image is selected in the step above)

5 The folder or individual image is opened within Local view. If a folder has been opened, the first image in the folder will be displayed, with its full filename path – i.e. where it is physically located – displayed at the top of the window above the image

Beware

If you are accessing images from an external device and the device is removed, the images on it will no longer be available in Local view. However, they will still be available if they have been copied to Cloud view.

6 Right-click on the image in the main window to access its menu. This can be used for a number of options, including copying the image to Cloud view, and also adding it to an album

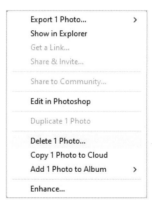

Don't forget

Individual images can also be copied to Cloud view by accessing them in the main window and clicking on the **Copy [ ] Photos to Cloud** button, as in Step 2 on page 39.

7 Move the cursor over the folder in the **Browse** section sidebar, click on the menu button, as in Step 3 on page 37, and click on the **Copy to Cloud** option to copy the whole folder to Cloud view

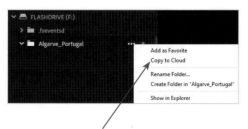

Starting with Cloud View

The Cloud view interface contains the same editing options as Local view, but there are significant differences in terms of storing and managing images, due to the cloud storage capabilities of this view. The main differences are in the sidebar.

The **Add Photos** button at the top of the Cloud view sidebar can be used to add images directly to Cloud view, without the need to copy them from Local view – see pages 44-46.

1 Click on the **Cloud** tab in the sidebar to access Cloud view

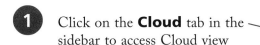

2 Click on a left-pointing arrowhead next to a category to expand it – e.g. the **All Photos** category

42

Cloud view should be thought of as the default option for editing images once they have been copied from Local view or added directly to Cloud view with the **Add Photos** button.

3 The sidebar area extends downward as each item is expanded

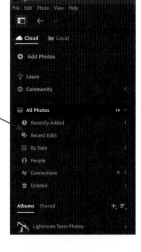

4 The **All Photos** section has a range of options for locating images and selecting which ones are displayed in the main window

5 Click on the **Learn** option to access **Lightroom Academy**, which contains a comprehensive range of help tools and tutorials for getting the most out of Lightroom

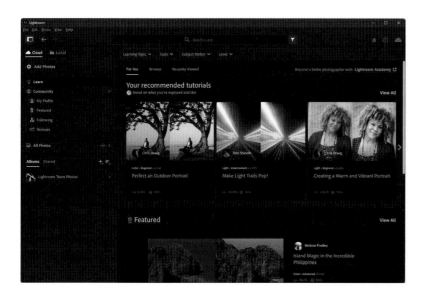

Don't forget

For more help options, see pages 30-32.

6 Click on the **Community** option to access the Lightroom community of connected users who share their images and editing techniques

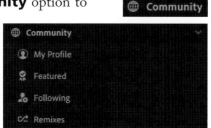

7 Use the **Albums** option at the bottom of the Cloud view sidebar to view existing albums and create more. Use the **Shared** tab to share your images

Don't forget

For more information about using albums and sharing images, see Chapter 10.

Adding Images in Cloud View

As shown on pages 40-41, it is possible to view more photos in Local view than just those stored on the computer that is being used to access them. In Cloud view, additional images can also be added without first having to access Local view to obtain them. There are various options for this.

Adding images from a folder
To add images from an entire folder on your computer:

1 Click on the **Add Photos** button at the top of the Cloud view sidebar

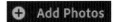

2 Click on a folder to select it

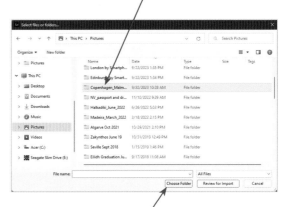

3 Click on the **Choose Folder** button

4 By default, all images in the folder are selected – i.e. the **Select All** button is checked **On**

Click in the box in the top left-hand corner of an image to deselect it – i.e. so that the checkmark is not showing – if you do not want to add the whole contents of a folder. If one image is deselected, the **Select All** option also becomes deselected.

5 Click on the **Add [ ] Items** button to add the folder contents to Cloud view

6 The images are available in the **Recently Added** section of **All Photos** in the Cloud view sidebar

Beware

It can take a few minutes to add all of the images from a folder, depending on their size and number.

Adding individual images
To add individually selected images:

1 Access the window in Step 2 on the previous page and double-click on a folder to open it. Select one image or more in the window, then click on the **Review for Import** button

Hot tip

To delete images from Cloud view, select one image or more in any view, then select **Edit** > **Delete [ ] Photos** from the top menu bar, or right-click on the selection and select the same option.

2 All of the selected images are displayed. If required, click on a checkbox to deselect an image so that there is no checkmark showing

3 Click on the **Add [ ] Photos** button to add the selected image(s) in the same way as for a folder

45

...cont'd

Adding images from a smartphone

Smartphones are now one of the most popular devices for capturing digital images. Within Lightroom it is possible to download these images so that they can be edited and managed.

Beware

Any images that have previously been downloaded from a smartphone onto the computer being used will not be available in the window in Step 3, even if they were not originally downloaded in Lightroom.

Hot tip

Images can also be opened from a smartphone in Local view, in a similar way to using Cloud view. To do this, click on the connected smartphone at the top of the Local view sidebar.

Select the required images in the main window and click on the **Choose folder** button to select a destination.

1 Connect your smartphone to your computer and click on the **Add Photos** button as in Step 1 on page 44

2 Click on the smartphone in the **Connected Devices** section

3 The images on the smartphone are displayed, with all of them selected by default

4 The connected device is shown in the top left-hand corner of the window

5 Click on the **Add [ ] Photos** button to add the selected images in the same way as for a folder and individual images

3 Lightroom Views

This chapter covers different ways in which you can view Lightroom images.

Photo Grid View

Lightroom has several options for how images are viewed in the main window.

Photo Grid view is only available in Cloud view and displays images in a non-symmetrical grid. To use it:

1 Click on the **Photo Grid** button from the collection of view buttons – see the first tip. The Photo Grid 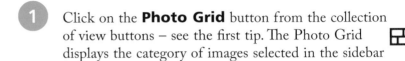 displays the category of images selected in the sidebar

2 Drag this slider at the bottom of the main window to change the magnification of the Photo Grid images

A lesser magnification enables more images to be viewed

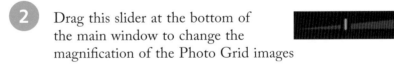

...cont'd

A greater magnification displays more detail for the images

3 Click on an image in Photo Grid view to select it

Don't forget

When an image is selected, in any view, this is indicated by a thin border around the image.

4 Click on these buttons at the bottom of the window to apply a rating to the selected image, which appears below the image

Hot tip

If ratings are applied, this can be one criterion for searching for images (see page 180).

Square Grid View

Square Grid view is available in both Cloud view and Local view, and it displays images in a symmetrical grid.

1 Click on the **Square Grid** button from the collection of view buttons. Square Grid view displays the category of images selected in the sidebar

2 Use the Magnification slider at the bottom of the window to change the magnification of the images

Hot tip

Use the maximum amount of zoom in Step 2 to view images for potential editing in Detail view.

3 The editing tools are available in the right-hand toolbar in Square Grid view. However, they cannot be used on the images in this view. Click on one of the editing tools to show or hide the Grid View panel. Click on the **Switch to Detail** button to view the images in this view, from where numerous editing options can be applied

The **Sort** options in Step 4 are also available in Photo Grid view in Cloud view.

4 Click on this button on the bottom toolbar (to the right of the collection of view buttons) to select an option for the order in which images are displayed in Square Grid view (**Sort**)

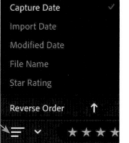

5 Click on an image to select it, and click on these buttons on the bottom toolbar to select the image as **Flag as Picked** or **Flag as Rejected**

The **Flag** options in Step 5 are also available in Photo Grid view in Cloud view.

51

Compare View

Compare view can be used to view two images next to each other, to check the quality of the images. It is also possible to edit individual images in Compare view. To use Compare view:

1 Click on the **Compare** button from the collection of view buttons

2 If the **Filmstrip** is not showing at the bottom of the Compare window, click on this button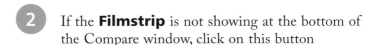

3 Click in the left-hand panel of Compare view, then click on an image in the Filmstrip at the bottom of the window to include it in the left-hand panel. Repeat the process for the right-hand panel

The Filmstrip is located below the selected images in Compare view (and also in Detail view). Each selected image is denoted by a down-pointing white arrow.

4 Click on one of the panels to zoom in on an image, without affecting the other image. Click again to zoom out on an image

5 Click on these buttons at the top of the Compare view window to change the orientation of the images being viewed – i.e. from Portrait mode to Landscape mode

6 Click on this button on the bottom toolbar so that the links become closed. This enables the same zoom magnification to be applied to both images in the Compare window at the same time

Don't forget

The orientation modes in Step 5 are most effective when viewing images in the same respective orientation.

Hot tip

Click on the **Fit** button on the bottom toolbar to access a range of magnification options.

53

...cont'd

Hot tip

If an image that is being edited in Local view has already been copied to Cloud view, click on the **Update edits to cloud** button at the top of the window to copy the edited version of the image to Cloud view too.

7 The editing controls are available in Compare view, located at the right-hand side of the window. Click on one of the images in Compare view to select it and apply any editing changes, as required. The changes are displayed in the main window

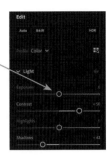

8 Click on this button on the bottom toolbar to return an edited image to its original state. Click on the button again to view the edited version

Detail View

Detail view is where you can access the full editing power of Lightroom to fine-tune your images just the way you want. To get started with Detail view:

1 Click on the **Detail** button from the collection of view buttons

2 Click on an image in the Filmstrip to view it in the main window. The editing controls are available down the right-hand side of Detail view (see pages 56-58)

3 Click on more images in the Filmstrip, in either landscape or portrait orientation, to view them in the main Detail window, ready for editing

Don't forget

Detail view has the same **Sort**, **Ratings**, and **Flag** options as for the Photo Grid and Square Grid view options.

55

Beware

Detail view does not have the Magnification slider that is available in the Photo Grid and Square Grid views. To change the magnification, click on an image in the main window, or select options from the **Fit** button on the bottom toolbar, as shown on page 53.

...cont'd

Don't forget

If you move the cursor over the buttons in the right-hand toolbar, a blue background appears and remains there while the cursor is over the button.

Don't forget

For a comprehensive look at the editing functions within the desktop version of Lightroom, see Chapters 6 and 7.

4 Click on this button in the editing panel to access the **Presets** options. These can be used to apply preset color templates to images

5 Click on this button in the editing panel to access the **Edit** options. These can be used to apply a range of light-editing and color-editing techniques to images

6 Click on this button in the editing panel to access the **Crop & Rotate** options. These can be used to crop out any unwanted areas of an image, and also to rotate them

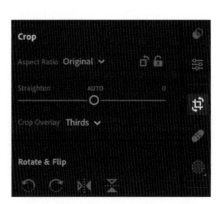

7 Click on this button in the editing panel to access the **Healing** options. These can be used to remove unwanted items in images, in either the foreground or the background

8 Click on this button in the editing panel to access the **Masking** options. These can be used to apply masks so that editing techniques can be applied to specific parts of an image

Click on the **Masking** button to view a pop-out version of the Masking options.

...cont'd

Hot tip

All of the editing options can be accessed by pressing their respective letters on the keyboard:

Shift + **P** for Presets.

E for Edit.

C for Crop & Rotate.

H for Healing.

M for Masking.

V for Versions.

⑨ Click on this button in the editing panel to access the **Versions** options. These can be used to create a new version of an image, with a unique name, for editing purposes

⑩ Click on this button in the editing panel to access general editing options and settings

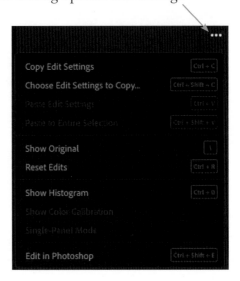

4 Quick Wins with Presets

Presets are collections of editing effects that can be applied to images in Lightroom in a single click. This chapter covers the presets that are already available in the app and how you can manage them, and also shows how to create your own presets.

About Presets

Editing the color elements of digital images can be a time-consuming process if you want to get them looking their best. However, in Lightroom there is an extensive range of preset editing options, where all of the work has already been done to create edits for all occasions. These can include:

- Landscape
- Architecture
- Portraits
- Night images
- Artistic effects

It is worth taking some time to explore the presets, as they can save a lot of time in the editing process in the long run.

Presets can be viewed and applied in **Compare** view and **Detail** view.

1 Different presets can dramatically change the appearance of an image, in a single click

2 Categories for different presets can be selected from the buttons above the thumbnail images of the presets, at the top of the **Presets** panel

Don't forget

Click here to access the Presets options. If you are in another editing section, move the cursor over the **Presets** button, which will appear blue.

3 Move the cursor over a preset thumbnail to view the effect on the image in the main window. Click on the thumbnail to apply the preset to the image

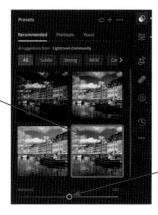

61

Hot tip

Once a preset has been selected, drag this slider to alter the amount of the preset effect.

4 Presets are a great way to quickly apply the same color-editing effects to similar types of images

Recommended Presets

The **Recommended** section of the Presets panel contains presets that have been created by other Lightroom users. These are then shared to Lightroom Community so that they can be used by other people. Presets that appear in the Recommended section are selected by Artificial Intelligence (AI) to make the most of images that you have added to Lightroom – AI analyzes your images and selects the best presets accordingly. To use Recommended presets:

Don't forget

For a detailed look at Lightroom Community, see pages 24-27.

62

1 Select an image in the main window and click on the **Recommended** tab at the top of the Presets panel

2 Since **Recommended** presets are selected by AI, an internet connection is required for them to be displayed. Therefore, they can only be accessed in Cloud view and not Local view, which displays this message in the Presets panel

3 Click on the **Cloud** tab at the top of the sidebar

4 AI suggestions for possible presets are displayed in the **Recommended** panel

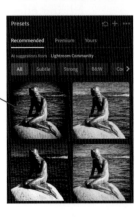

5 Move the cursor over a preset to preview it for the image in the main window. Click on the **More like this** button to view similar presets

Don't forget

Click on a preset to apply it to the image in the main window. Click on this button at the right-hand side of the bottom toolbar to view the original version of an image once a preset has been applied. Click on the button again to display the preset version:

6 A **Similar to** button is added to the top of the Presets panel, with the relevant presets in the panel below

7 Click on the **X** symbol on the **Similar to** button to close these options

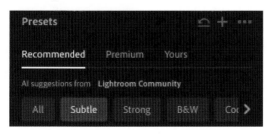

8 If you select another option from the buttons at the top of the **Recommended** panel, the **Similar to** option will no longer be available

Saving Recommended Presets

It is possible to save Recommended presets so that you can use them at any time, not just when you are in Cloud view. You can also edit a Recommended preset to customize it just how you want it. To save Recommended presets:

1 Move the cursor over the required preset and click on the menu button (three dots) in the right-hand corner of the thumbnail image

2 Click on the **Save to your presets...** option

3 Enter a name for the new preset and click on the **Save** button

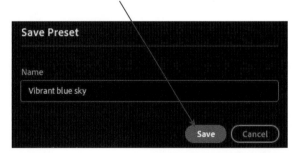

Don't forget

Presets in the **Yours** panel can be accessed in either Local view or Cloud view.

4 Click on the **Yours** tab in the Presets panel

5 Click on the right-pointing arrowhead next to **Saved from Community** to view the preset that has been saved

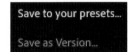

Editing a preset

To edit a preset that you have saved from the Recommended section, as shown on the previous page:

1 Click on the preset in the **Yours** panel and click on the **Edit** button in the sidebar, directly below the **Presets** button

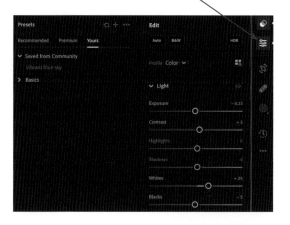

If the **Edit** panel is activated, the **Presets** panel moves to the left if it is activated too.

2 The editing options are displayed in the **Edit** panel. Drag on the sliders to change the effect of the preset, as required

For a detailed look at the **Edit** options in desktop Lightroom, see Chapter 6.

3 Right-click on the preset and click on the **Update with Current Settings** option to save the edited preset

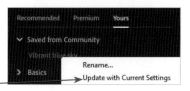

Editing and updating an existing preset can be a good way of fine-tuning it to make it appear exactly the way that you want.

Premium Presets

The **Premium** section of the Presets panel contains presets that are included with the Creative Cloud subscription version of Lightroom. These are grouped into specific categories, and some of them can be used to apply a preset to one component of an image, such as the sky or the face of a person in a portrait.

1 Select an image in the main window and click on the **Premium** tab at the top of the Presets panel

2 Click on the right-pointing arrowhead next to a category

3 The category is expanded, showing all of the Premium presets within it. Click on one to apply it to the image

Don't forget

Once a preset has been selected, drag the slider below it to change the amount of the effect.

4 Select a Premium preset that applies to a specific component of an image – i.e. the sky, in this case. The preset is applied to the relevant component (above)

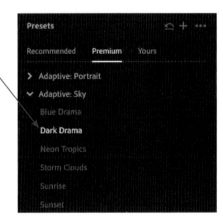

5 Select another preset to see how it changes the relevant component in the image

Hot tip

Some of the options in the Premium presets, which apply to a specific component in an image, include Portraits, Seasons, Food, Landscape, Travel, and Urban Architecture.

Yours Presets

The **Yours** section of the Presets panel contains presets that have been saved there from the Recommended section (**Saved from Community**), and also the standard default presets that are included with Lightroom. To use these presets:

1 Select an image in the main window and click on the **Yours** tab at the top of the Presets panel

2 Click on the right-pointing arrowhead next to **Saved from Community** to view any presets that have been saved from the Recommended section

3 Click on the right-pointing arrowhead next to **Basics** (and the categories within it) to view the standard Lightroom presets

4 As with other presets, move the cursor over a preset to preview the effect on the image, and click on the preset to apply it

Don't forget

Once a preset has been previewed for an image, a text box appears above the image's thumbnail on the Filmstrip, indicating which preset is being used.

Deleting a preset

Presets in the **Saved from Community** section are the only ones that can be deleted from the Presets section. This is because they have been created within Lightroom from another preset, rather than being included with the app. Presets in the **Saved from Community** section can be thought of as your own customized presets and they can therefore be managed slightly differently from other presets. To delete a preset from the **Saved from Community** section:

1 Right-click on a preset that has been saved to the **Saved from Community** section and click on the **Delete...** option

Hot tip

Click on the **Manage Presets** option in Step 1 or Step 3 to access options for showing or hiding the options in the Presets panel – see page 78 for details.

2 Click on the **Delete** button to confirm the action

Permanently Delete Preset?

Are you sure you want to delete preset "Vibrant blue sky"?

You cannot undo this action. Deleted presets are removed from all synced devices.

Delete   Cancel

3 If any of the presets in the Recommended or Premium section are right-clicked on, as in Step 1, the **Delete...** option is not available on the menu

Hide "Portraits: Deep Skin"

Manage Presets

Reset Hidden Presets

69

Using Presets

To get started with presets and access the considerable possibilities that are on offer:

1 In either **Compare** view or **Detail** view, select an image, and click on the **Presets** button on the right-hand toolbar

2 Click on the **Recommended** tab

3 Click on the **All** button

4 Move the cursor over one of the **Presets** options to preview it in both the thumbnail and the image in the main window

Hot tip

Click on the menu button on the thumbnail in Step 4 to access options for saving the preset, either as an original in your own preset section or as a new version.

Save to your presets...

Save as Version...

5 Click on a preset thumbnail to apply it to the image in the main window, indicated by a blue border around the thumbnail

Beware

Whenever a new image is chosen in the main window when **Presets** has been selected, it is analyzed by Lightroom to ensure the preset effect is the best possible option. This can take a few seconds or more, depending on the power of your computer.

71

6 Drag the slider below the selected preset thumbnail to increase or decrease the amount of the preset effect

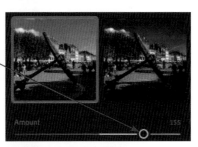

Beware

If consecutive presets are applied to the same image, this is done using the original in each case, not the previously selected preset version of the image.

Creating Presets

In addition to the presets that are included with Lightroom, you can also create and save your own presets. To do this:

1 In the Presets panel, click on the **+** button, or click on the menu button (three dots) and click on the **Create Preset...** option

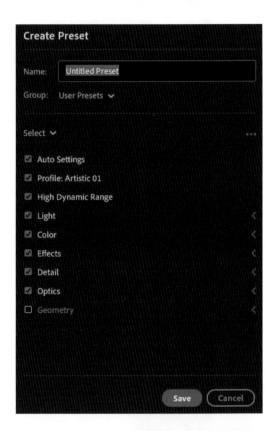

2 Options for the preset are available in the **Create Preset** panel

Color elements of a new preset can be fine-tuned once the preset has been created – see page 65 for details.

3 Click in the **Name** text box and type a unique name for the preset

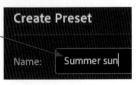

4 Check the general settings options **On** or **Off** at the top of the panel

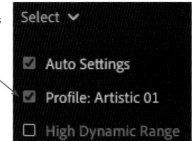

Hot tip

Click on the **Select** option in Step 4 to access options for groups of items to include or exclude in new presets.

5 For the color options for the preset, click on the left-pointing arrow next to a category to expand it

6 For each color category, check items **On** or **Off** as required for the preset

7 Click on the **Save** button in Step 2 on the previous page to create the preset

Save

8 By default, the new preset is available in the newly created **User Presets** group in the **Yours** section

73

...cont'd

9 Click on the preset to apply it to the currently selected image. Click on the **Edit** button in the right-hand toolbar to view full color elements for the preset

Don't forget

The newly created preset can be used without accessing the options in the **Edit** panel. However, this can give greater flexibility for creating it exactly as you want.

10 Make any light-editing and color-editing changes as required by dragging the appropriate sliders

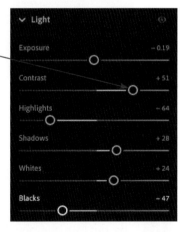

11 Right-click on the preset to select from these options: **Rename...** to rename the preset; **Update with Current Settings** (if it has

been edited, as above); or **Move To Group** to move it to another group within the Presets panel

Creating Groups for Presets

Presets can be put into their own groups, which can be created at the same time as creating a new preset. To do this:

1 Access the **Create Preset** panel, as shown on page 72, and click on the

down-pointing arrowhead next to the current group

2 Click on the **New Group...** option

3 Enter a name for the new group in the **Name** text box

4 Click on the **Create** button

5 Create a new preset, with the new group name

6 The new group is added to the **Yours** section in the Presets panel, with the newly created preset included

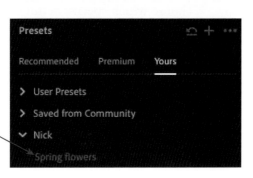

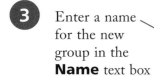

The default group for new presets is **User Presets**, which is where new presets will be placed if no other group is selected or created.

Presets that you have created can be moved to other groups by right-clicking on a preset and selecting **Move To Group** from the menu that appears, then selecting a new destination group (or the **New Group** option). However, pre-installed presets cannot be moved in this way.

Copying to Multiple Images

Presets cannot be applied directly to a range of images – i.e. more than one. However, it is possible to copy the settings for a preset and then apply these to a group of selected images. To do this:

1 In **Detail** view, apply a preset to an image

Any editing settings that have been applied can be copied to multiple images in the way shown on these two pages, not just those from presets.

2 Click on the **Copy Edit Settings** button at the bottom of the window to copy all of the settings used in the preset

3 Or, click on the gear icon in Step 2 and choose which specific settings to copy by checking the relevant checkboxes **On** or **Off**, then click on the **Copy** button

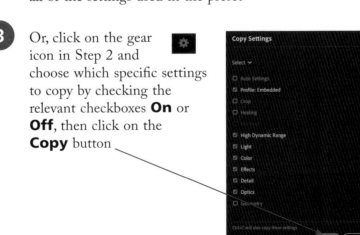

4 Once the settings have been copied, in either Step 2 or Step 3 on the previous page, access either **Photo Grid** or **Square Grid** view. The image with the preset is displayed. Select other images as required

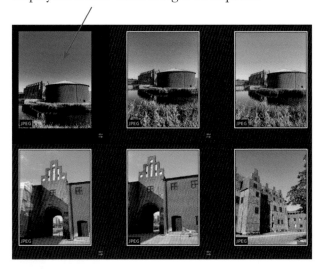

5 Click on the **Paste Edit Settings** button at the bottom of the window

6 The settings from the preset are applied to all of the selected images

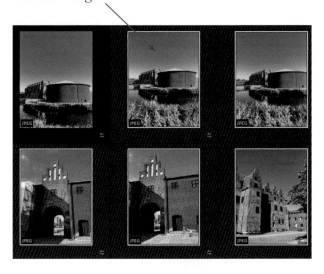

Don't forget

When images are selected in either Photo Grid or Square Grid view, this is indicated by a thin white border around the images.

Managing Presets

There are dozens of different presets available in Lightroom, and for most people only a small number will be used on a regular basis. It is possible to manage presets so that only the categories in which you are most interested are displayed. To do this:

1 In either the Premium or the Yours section, right-click on a preset and click on the **Manage Presets** option, or click on the menu button (three dots) at the top of the Presets panel and select the same option

Presets in the **Recommended** section cannot be managed and turned **Off** in the same way as those in the **Premium** and **Yours** sections.

2 For both Premium presets (right) and Yours presets (below), check **Off** any categories that are not required (so that the checkmark is not showing). These categories will no longer be visible in the respective panels. Check the categories back **On** if you want to make them visible and use them

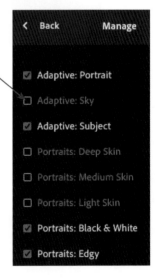

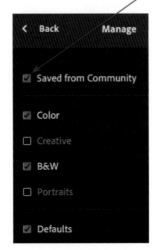

5 Using Profiles

Similar to presets, profiles can be used to quickly apply a range of editing functions.

About Profiles and Presets

In terms of their operation, profiles and presets in Lightroom perform a similar visual task – they can change the overall appearance of an image by selecting a single option. However, there are subtle differences between the two functions, which can be thought of in this way:

- **Profiles** are applied in a similar way to those that are created when an image is captured – when digital images are captured, they have a color profile applied to them by the device on which they are produced. In Lightroom, profiles are applied to the same elements as those created when the image is captured. For this reason, Lightroom profiles are particularly effective for editing images captured in the RAW file format, but they do not have to be used exclusively in this way.

- **Presets** are applied to the existing color profile that is already created with the image, like a layer above it.

One way to see the difference between profiles and presets is to view the editing options once each function has been applied.

- When a new profile has been applied to an image, the editing controls are not altered – i.e. they are still in their default positions – and additional editing can be applied, effectively on top of changes made by the profile.

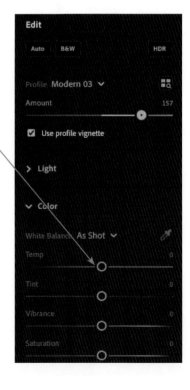

- When a preset has been applied, the editing controls are altered by the elements of the preset. The editing controls can then be manipulated to change the appearance of the preset. Images with presets also have a profile associated with them, which, by default, is the one that is created when the image was captured. This is displayed at the top of the **Edit** panel.

The default color profiles are **Color** or **Monochrome**, unless an image has been captured in RAW format – see pages 84-85.

In general, it is best to use profiles at the beginning of the editing process to create a consistent foundation for subsequent editing changes, or at the end of the editing process to create a uniformed appearance and style for your edited images.

Accessing Profiles

Profiles can be applied to images in Compare and Detail view at any point of the editing process. To do this:

1 Select an image in **Compare** or **Detail** view and click on the **Edit** button in the right-hand toolbar

2 The default color profile is shown here, next to the **Profile** option

Hot tip

Editing changes can be made to an image before or after a profile has been applied. Any editing changes work in conjunction with the profile; they do not override it.

82

3 The **Edit** settings are not affected by the selected profile – i.e. they all remain at 0

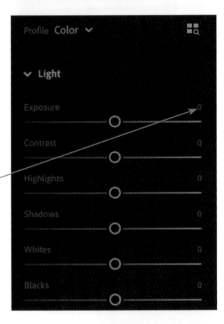

4 Click on the current profile to access more options. Click on the **Browse All Profiles...** option or click on this button at the top of the **Edit** window

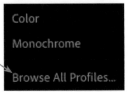

5 The two default options (**Color** and **Monochrome**) are displayed at the top of the Profile panel, in the **Favorites** section, with the rest of the categories below them

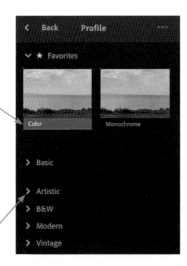

6 Click on a right-pointing arrowhead to expand a category. The profiles are displayed as thumbnails below the category heading

7 Click on a profile to apply it to the selected image

8 Drag the slider to change the amount of the profile, as required

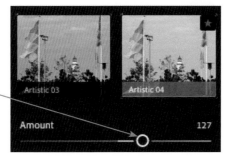

Don't forget

Click on the **Back** button at the top of the Profile panel to return to the main Edit panel.

The selected profile is displayed at the top of the panel, with no change to the editing settings.

83

RAW File Profiles

When digital images are captured by a digital camera or a smartphone, they are usually automatically converted into a specific file format. This is frequently JPEG (Joint Photographic Experts Group) or JPG, which is a versatile file format that is designed primarily for displaying images online, although it is also now popular for printed images. Another popular file format for online use is PNG (Portable Network Group), while TIFF (Tagged Image File Format) is widely used for printed images.

When a digital image is converted into a specific file format, certain default editing functions are applied to the image. This is done primarily to prepare the image for its final output method. However, a popular option for photographers is to capture images without any processing being applied to the image. This is known as a RAW image – i.e. it is the raw data as captured by the device, without any processing applied. RAW files contain uncompressed data that is usually converted by specific devices to their own versions of the RAW file format – e.g. Nikon has its own RAW file format (Nikon Electric File/NEF), as does Canon (CRW).

The great advantage of RAW images is that you can edit every element of images, without any previous editing having been applied to them. In Lightroom there is a range of profiles that are available when a RAW image is being viewed and edited. This can be used at any point of the editing process, to apply a range of editing effects to the RAW image. To use RAW profiles:

Don't forget

RAW is not an acronym, just an indication that no other file format is being produced for images captured in this way.

Beware

RAW profiles are not available if the selected image is in a specific file format – e.g. JPEG.

1 Select an image in the RAW format in either **Compare** or **Detail** view

2 Access the **Browse All Profiles** section, as shown on page 82. The standard profiles are available, but the RAW ones are included at the top of the panel (these also appear in the **Favorites** section)

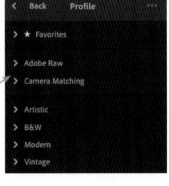
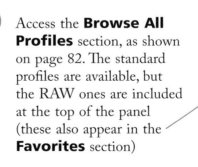

...cont'd

3 Click on the right-pointing arrowhead next to the **Adobe Raw** section to expand it. This contains profiles used for the Adobe RAW file format. Click on a profile, as required, to apply it to the selected image

An increasing number of smartphones can capture RAW images, particularly high-end models.

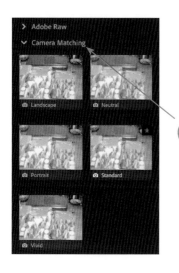

4 Click on the right-pointing arrowhead next to the **Camera Matching** section to expand it. This contains profiles specific to the device on which the image was captured. Click on a profile, as required, to apply it to the selected image

Lightroom can identify the type of device used to capture an image from the metadata that is included when the image is taken.

5 Click on the **Back** button at the top of the **Profile** panel to return to the main **Edit** panel. The RAW profile is displayed at the top of the panel, with no editing changes made to the Edit settings at this point

85

Managing Profiles

There are certain options for how items in the Profiles panel are displayed. To use these:

1 Click on the menu button (three dots) at the top of the **Browse All Profiles** panel, as shown on page 83

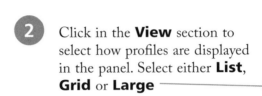

2 Click in the **View** section to select how profiles are displayed in the panel. Select either **List**, **Grid** or **Large**

Hot tip

The **Large** option in Step 2 is the best way to view the effect of a profile, but it does take up more space on the screen.

3 Click in the **Type** section to select which types of profiles are displayed. Select from **All**, **Color** or **B&W** (Black & White)

4 Click on the **Manage Profiles** option to select which categories of profiles are displayed

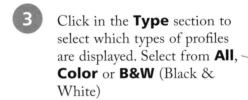

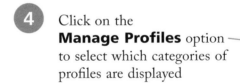

5 Check the categories **On** or **Off**, as required

Beware

If a selected image is not a RAW one, the **Adobe Raw** and **Camera Matching** options in Step 5 are replaced by the **Basic** category.

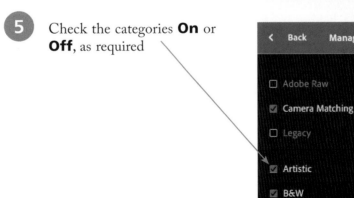

6 Edit Options

Editing digital images is at the heart of Lightroom, and this chapter takes a comprehensive look at the tools and functions on offer, from editing color in images to applying effects such as vignetting.

Accessing Edit Tools

Editing color elements of images is one of the primary functions of Lightroom, and this can be done with great sophistication with the **Edit** tools. These can all be accessed from the toolbar at the right-hand side of the Lightroom window, in Compare or Detail view. To get started with the **Edit** tools:

Don't forget

Generally, it is best to perform editing tasks in Detail view, as the selected image will be shown at a larger size.

1 Select an image in either **Compare** or **Detail** view. The editing tools are located on the right-hand toolbar

Don't forget

The Edit tools can be used in conjunction with the Presets options – i.e. if the Presets panel is open, it remains so when the Edit option is selected. However, if one of the other editing options is selected, the Presets panel closes.

2 Click on the **Edit** button to access the full range of color-editing options. Use the buttons at the top of the **Edit** panel to, from left to right: apply automatic color-editing settings (**Auto**); convert an image to black and white (**B&W**); and apply High Dynamic Range effects to an image (**HDR**)

Hot tip

High Dynamic Range (HDR) effects can improve the tonal appearance of an image and also make colors more vivid.

3 The **Edit** panel contains numerous color-editing options, in different categories

4 Click on the right-pointing arrowhead next to one of the **Edit** categories to expand it

5 All of the **Edit** categories can be expanded at the same time, if required

Beware

If several of the **Edit** categories are expanded, you may have to scroll down the screen to view all of them and their contents.

Hot tip

Some of the **Edit** categories have sub-categories within them. If these are available, click on the left-pointing arrowhead to access them.

Histogram

The Histogram is a function that is used with digital images to display the tonal distribution of colors in an image, using a graph that shows the red, green, and blue color channels in the image. This can then be used as the basis for making editing changes, depending on what is displayed in the Histogram. To access and use the Histogram:

Don't forget

The horizontal axis of the Histogram denotes the darkest area (pure black) of the image at the far left-hand side of the graph. From left to right, it moves through shadows, midtones, and highlights to the lightest part of the image (pure white). The peaks of the graph illustrate the distribution of the color tones at that point. The ideal distribution of the graph depends on the type of image that you want to produce.

1 Select **View** >
Edit Panels >
Histogram from
the top menu bar

2 The **Histogram**
is displayed at the
top of the Edit panel,
showing the tonal
distribution of the red,
green, and blue color
channels in the image

3 As editing changes are
made to the image,
such as **Exposure**,
Contrast, and
Highlights, these
are displayed in
the Histogram, in
real time

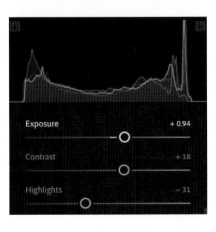

Clipping

One of the main uses for the Histogram is to identify and potentially rectify areas in an image that are over-exposed or under-exposed, which results in a loss of definition in the affected area. This is known as clipping and occurs at the extremes of highlights (over-exposed) and shadows (under-exposed). The Histogram can be used to identify these areas, and the editing tools can then be used to improve their clarity. To do this:

1 Right-click (Windows) or **Ctrl** + click (Mac) on the Histogram and check **On** the options for **Show Clipping in Photo**, **Show Clipping in Histogram**, and **Show Clipping in Photo on Hover**

Once **Show Clipping in Histogram** has been turned **On** in Step 1, click on the arrows at the top of the Histogram to show or hide clipping overlays in the image.

2 Any clipping in the image is displayed: red overlay for highlights (over-exposed) and blue overlay for shadows (under-exposed)

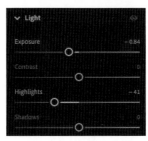

3 Drag the editing sliders to rectify the clipped areas. This is usually done with the **Exposure**, **Contrast**, **Highlights**, and **Shadows** controls. As changes are made, they are displayed on the image

When performing editing actions to remove clipping, this will impact the rest of the image, which may produce an unsatisfactory overall effect. One way to avoid this is to apply a mask to the area affected by clipping. See pages 126-131 for more details about masking.

4 Perform editing actions until the clipped areas do not display any red or blue overlays. In some cases, if there is not enough definition in an area it will remain over-exposed or under-exposed

Light Edit Options

Within the Edit section there are several options that can be used to fine-tune the color elements of an image. The first of these are the Light options. To use these:

Another option, at the bottom of the Light panel, is the Curve graph. This can be used to edit the red, green, and blue color channels (or all of them together) of the highlights and shadows regions in an image. Drag on the graph line to edit the color elements in the image, which appear in real time.

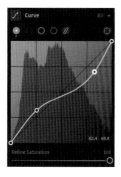

Experiment with the Light editing effects. If you do not like any effect, drag the slider back to the 0 setting.

1 Select an image in either **Compare** or **Detail** view and click on the **Edit** button

2 Click on the right-pointing arrowhead next to the **Light** option to expand the panel

3 The **Light** editing options are displayed. These are: **Exposure**; **Contrast**; **Highlights**; **Shadows**; **Whites**; and **Blacks**. At this point, the sliders for each option are set to 0

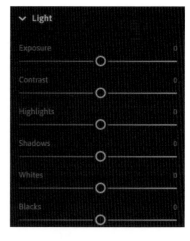

...cont'd

4 Click on the **Auto** button at the top of the Edit panel to apply automatic settings. When this is done, the sliders in the Light panel are altered accordingly

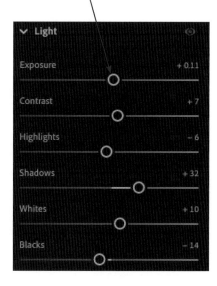

Image editing is very subjective, so if you like a certain editing effect, then stick with it.

5 Drag the sliders as required to apply further editing changes to the image. The greater the amount of change to the sliders, the more dramatic the editing effect

Click on this button on the bottom toolbar to toggle between the original image and the edited version:

Color Edit Options

The Color editing options can be used to apply a range of changes to the color elements of an image. To do this:

1 Select an image in either **Compare** or **Detail** view, then click on the **Edit** button

Don't forget

The functionality for the **Color Mixer**, **Point Color**, and **Color Grading** options are accessed by clicking on the left-pointing arrowhead next to them – see pages 96-99 for details.

2 Click on the right-pointing arrowhead next to the **Color** option to expand the panel

3 The **Color** editing options are displayed. These are: **White Balance**; **Temp**; **Tint**; **Vibrance**; **Saturation**; **Color Mixer**; **Point Color**; and **Color Grading**. At this point, the sliders for each option are set to 0

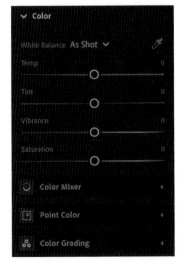

Don't forget

White balance refers to the process of displaying white in an image as accurately as possible so that it matches white in the real world as it was captured. If the white balance is not accurate, the image may appear with a strange color-cast effect.

4 Click on the down-pointing arrowhead next to the **White Balance** option and select an item as required

5 Click on the Eye Dropper icon next to the

White Balance box to select an area of the image that can be set as the white point in the image. Click on an appropriate area; all other color-editing functions will be applied based on this being the white point of the image

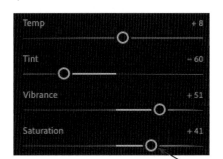

Don't forget

The area in the large circle in Step 5 displays a magnified version of the area beneath the dropper so that an accurate selection can be made.

6 Drag the sliders, as required, to apply color-editing changes to the image

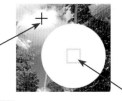

7 The color changes can be as subtle or as dramatic as you want

Hot tip

Double-click on the circle on any of the sliders to return the value to 0. This applies for all of the editing functions.

...cont'd

Color Mixer

The Color Mixer option can be used to edit the appearance of whole groups of colors. To do this:

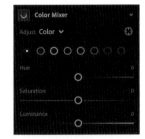

1 Click on the right-pointing arrowhead next to the **Color Mixer** option to expand the panel

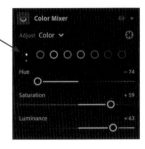

2 Click on the **Adjust** option to select which item will be edited – e.g. specific colors or other elements in an image; see the Don't forget tip

In image editing, hue refers to color families of primary and secondary colors – i.e. blue, green, orange, red, violet, and yellow; saturation refers to the level of intensity of a color; and luminance refers to the brightness of a color. If any of these options are selected in Step 2, color sliders will be available for each color and can be edited for the selected item.

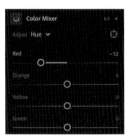

3 For the **Color** option, click on a color and drag the **Hue**, **Saturation**, and **Luminance** sliders to adjust the settings for the selected color. The edit changes apply to the selected color in the image, while the other colors remain unchanged

...cont'd

The Color Mixer option can also be used directly on an image:

1 Click on this icon at the top right-hand side of the **Color Mixer** panel

2 A pop-out **Target Adjustment** panel is displayed on the image. Click and hold on the bar at the left-hand side of the panel to drag it into a different position. Click on either **Hue**, **Saturation**, or **Luminance** to edit that element of the image

3 Click on a color within an image. A color bar is displayed. Drag left or right on the bar to edit the item selected in Step 2

4 The editing change is displayed on the image as you drag on the color bar

When you click and hold on the left-hand bar in Step 2, the pop-out panel displays a blue border around it, indicating that it can be moved by dragging it.

The two buttons below the color bar in Step 4 show the range for how much the selected color can be edited.

...cont'd

Point Color

The Point Color option can be used to select a specific color in an image, rather than a whole color family as with the Color Mixer option on page 97. To do this:

Hot tip

The Point Color editing option changes all occurrences of a color, wherever it appears in the image. However, for more precise editing of a color with Point Color, a mask can be applied to a specific area of an image so that only the elements within that area will have the editing action applied to them. For more information about adding masks, see pages 126-131.

1 Click on the right-pointing arrowhead next to the **Point Color** option to expand the panel. Click on the Eye Dropper icon

2 Click on a specific color with the Eye Dropper. The color is displayed in a large circle

3 The selected color is displayed at the top of the Point Color panel. Click here to expand the panel

4 Use the sliders to edit the selected color, or drag on the color window and bars at the top of the panel. In the color window, drag horizontally to change the hue, drag vertically to change the saturation, and drag on the right-hand bar to change the luminance. As changes are made, the sliders are adjusted automatically, and the bottom bar displays a before-and-after version of the selected color and any changes that have been made

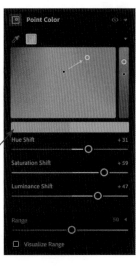

Color Grading

The Color Grading option can be used to create an overall stylistic effect for images. This can then be applied to several images, to create a consistent color effect. To do this:

1 Click on the right-pointing arrowhead next to the **Color Grading** option to expand the panel

2 Drag on the color circles to amend the overall color effects for **Midtones**, **Shadows**, and **Highlights**

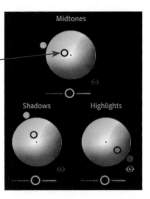

3 Drag the sliders for each item to change the amount of the effect for the currently selected colors

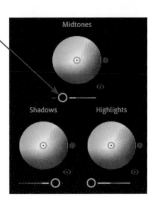

Hot tip

Color Grading is frequently used when editing movies, to create a consistent color style between scenes.

Don't forget

Click on these buttons at the top of the Color Grading panel to select specific options, from left to right: all editing options; Shadows; Midtones; Highlights; and Global, for editing all options within a single color wheel:

Don't forget

To copy a Color Grading effect to another image(s), click on the **Copy Edit Settings** button on the bottom toolbar, select another image(s) and click on the **Paste Edit Settings** button.

Effects Edit Options

The Effects editing options can be used to apply a range of effects to the overall look of an image. To use these:

1 Select an image in either **Compare** or **Detail** view, then click on the **Edit** button

2 Click on the right-pointing arrowhead next to the **Effects** option to expand the panel

100

Texture

The Texture effect can be used to add more definition to an image.

1 To see the full effect of the Texture option, zoom in on an image to see its detail

2 Drag the **Texture** slider to apply the effect

3 If a positive Texture effect is applied, the image can appear clearer and more defined. Return to 100% magnification to see the overall effect

Clarity

The Clarity effect can be used to make images appear more sharply in focus.

1 To see the full effect of the Clarity option, zoom in on an image to see its detail

2 Drag the **Clarity** slider to apply the effect

If a negative Clarity effect is applied, the image will appear more blurred.

3 If a positive Clarity effect is applied, the image can appear more clearly in focus, with a general sharpness

...cont'd

Dehaze

The Dehaze effect can be used to add more clarity to an image that appears hazy due to the light or weather conditions.

1 Open an image that has a hazy effect

2 Drag the **Dehaze** slider to apply the effect

3 If a positive Dehaze effect is applied, the haze is removed to make the overall image clearer

Vignette

The Vignette effect can be used to add an elliptical border to an image, in either white or black.

1 Open an image to which you want to add a Vignette effect

2 Drag the **Vignette** slider to apply the effect

3 Click on the left-pointing arrowhead to expand the Vignette panel and access more options for the Vignette effect

4 Drag the sliders to apply the effect on the image, which appears from the corners and along the edge of the image, depending on the amount that is applied

Hot tip

Drag the Vignette slider to the left to apply a darker effect, and drag it to the right to add a lighter effect.

Don't forget

The final Effects option is the Grain effect, which can be used to create a "speckled" effect on an image. If enough of the effect is applied, the image can take on the appearance of an impressionist painting.

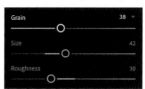

Detail Edit Options

The Detail editing options can be used to improve the overall clarity and sharpness of an image, using two main techniques – sharpening and noise reduction:

Sharpening works by increasing the contrast between individual pixels in an image, which can create an overall effect of making the image appear more clearly in focus.

1 In the **Detail** panel, click on the left-pointing arrowhead next to the **Sharpening** option to expand this

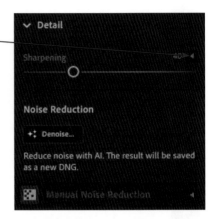

2 Drag the **Sharpening**, **Radius**, **Detail**, and **Masking** sliders to apply these effects, which can make an image appear more in focus

Noise in a digital image can appear when individual pixels are misrepresented in terms of the intended color in the image – i.e. they stand out from other pixels around them.

3 Click on the **Denoise**... button in the **Noise Reduction** section to remove any unwanted random color specks in the image. Expand the **Manual Noise Reduction** option to access sliders for removing noise

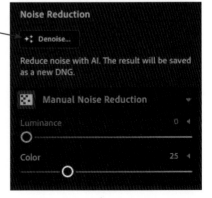

Optics Edit Options

The Optics editing options can be used to remove lens errors that occur when digital images are captured, and also color defringing, where the border between two colors can becomes distorted, creating an unwanted aberration along the edge of adjoining borders of color. To use the Optics option:

1 In the Optics panel, check **On** the **Remove Chromatic Aberration** checkbox

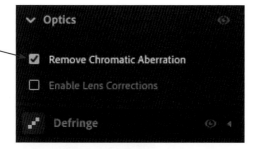

2 Click on the left-pointing arrowhead next to the **Defringe** option in Step 1 to expand the panel. Use the options to select colors to defringe and also the amount to be applied

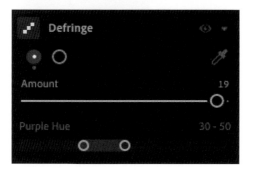

3 Check **On** the **Enable Lens Corrections** checkbox in the **Optics** panel. Expand the **Enable Lens Corrections** panel and use the sliders to amend any lens distortion in the image, as required

Defringing changes are usually quite subtle, so are not particularly obvious to the naked eye, but they can improve the overall appearance of an image.

Once the **Enable Lens Corrections** checkbox has been checked **On**, in Step 3, click on the left-pointing arrowhead to expand the panel.

Make lens corrections in small amounts so as not to over-correct the distortion.

Lens Blur Edit Options

The Lens Blur editing options can be used to blur the background behind a subject, to give it more prominence. To do this:

1 Select an image with a clear main subject

Hot tip

In traditional photography, the effect shown here is known as Depth of Field, which is achieved with the camera settings when an image is captured.

2 Expand the **Lens Blur** panel and check **On** the **Apply** checkbox to apply the effect

3 Drag the **Blur Amount** slider to increase or decrease the amount of the effect that is applied to the image

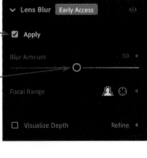

...cont'd

Editing Lens Blur

There are options for editing and fine-tuning the Lens Blur effect.

1 Click on the left-pointing arrowhead to expand the **Blur Amount** panel, and click on one of the options to change the blur effect

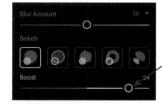

Drag the **Boost** slider in Step 1 to alter the lighting effect of the blurred area.

2 Click on the left-pointing arrowhead to expand the **Focal Range** option, and drag on this slider to alter the area to which the blur effect is applied. The area changes in the image as you drag the slider

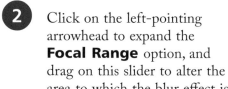

The **Focal Range** icon in Step 3 is located at the top right of the Focal Range panel.

3 Click on this icon in the **Focal Range** panel and drag on the image to manually create a focal range area

4 The focal range area selected in the previous step is the one that remains in focus, with the background blurred

The focal range area selected in Step 3 is denoted by a rectangle with a black and white border. The full focal area extends up the image from where the box is drawn.

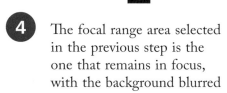

107

...cont'd

5 Check **On** the
Visualize Depth
checkbox to apply

a color overlay to the image, showing the focal areas.
Darker colors are blurred areas, while lighter colors are
more in focus

Hot tip

When either the **Focus**
or **Blur** options are
selected in Step 6, this
is indicated by a white
border around the
button. Only one option
can be selected at a
time, and the editing
effect is then applied to
that item accordingly.

6 Click on the left-
pointing **Refine**
arrowhead in the
previous step to expand
the **Visualize Depth**
panel. Click on the
Focus or **Blur** buttons
at the top of the
panel to apply editing
effects to the main
subject (**Focus**) or the
background (**Blur**)

7 Make selections accordingly in the panel for manually altering the focus area of the main subject or blurring areas in the image

8 Drag on the image with the selections made above to apply the effect. The colors change as the effect is being applied, with darker colors denoting blurred areas and lighter colors denoting areas more sharply in focus

The **Focus** or **Blur** options can be used without activating Visualize Depth. However, with it, it can be more effective to see exactly where in an image an effect is being applied.

9 Check **Off** the **Visualize Depth** checkbox to view the effect on the image, over the area selected in the previous step

Geometry Edit Options

The Geometry editing options can be used to change a range of features in an image, connected with its rotation and perspective. One of these features is to straighten subjects in an image with the Guided Upright option.

1 Select an image to which you want to make geometrical changes – e.g. straighten a subject in an image, in this case

Digital cameras and smartphone cameras often produce some form of distortion, particularly with tall buildings.

2 Expand the **Geometry** panel to view the options that can be applied

3 Click next to the **Upright** option to make selections for editing the perspective of the image

4 Click on the **Guided** option, or click on this button at the top right-hand side of the Geometry panel

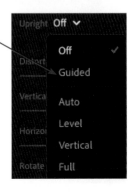

5 Drag the two guide lines vertically on the image. These are used to realign the perspective of the main subject

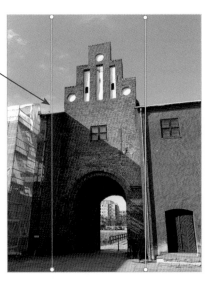

6 Click on this button to apply the effect

Hot tip

Drag the vertical lines in Step 5 to move them and change the editing effect applied by the Guided Upright process. Experiment with the lines in different locations to see the effect that they produce.

7 In most cases, the image will need to be cropped with the **Crop** editing tool to remove any space that has appeared during the change of perspective. Crop the image to create the final effect

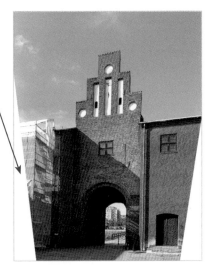

Don't forget

For more details about cropping images, see pages 118-119.

...cont'd

The rest of the Geometry effects can be achieved by dragging the appropriate sliders.

Distortion

Drag the **Distortion** slider to achieve an effect as if the image was being pushed or pulled from its middle.

Vertical

Drag the **Vertical** slider to change the perspective along the vertical plane of the image.

Horizontal

Drag the **Horizontal** slider to change the perspective along the horizontal plane of the image.

Rotate

Drag the **Rotate** slider to rotate the image either clockwise or anti-clockwise.

Applying a small degree of rotation can be used to straighten objects in an image.

...cont'd

Aspect

Drag the **Aspect** slider to create a portrait effect (drag to the right) or landscape effect (drag to the left) for the image.

There are also **X Offset** and **Y Offset** Geometry options. These can be used to move an image left or right or up and down respectively. These leave a white space when the offset effect is applied.

Scale

Drag the **Scale** slider to the right to expand the image from the center.

If you drag the **Scale** slider to the left, it will shrink the image, leaving a white border.

7 Manipulating Images

This chapter covers more ways in which images can be edited and manipulated, from cropping to masking specific areas for editing.

Don't forget

Most images benefit from some degree of cropping being applied to them.

Don't forget

For more details about using the **Crop & Rotate** and the **Healing** options, see pages 118-119 and 120-125 respectively.

More Editing Tools

In addition to the color-editing tools detailed in Chapter 6, Lightroom has a range of other tools that can be used to manipulate and enhance images in a variety of ways. Like the color-editing tools, these are accessed from the right-hand toolbar in either Compare view or Detail view.

Crop & Rotate

Click on the **Crop & Rotate** button to access options for cropping, rotating, or flipping an image. There are various cropping options to remove unwanted areas of an image to make the main subject more prominent and stand out more.

Healing

Click on the **Healing** button to access options for removing unwanted elements in an image, in various ways. This can be done by selecting the unwanted elements, and the Healing feature then covers them up.

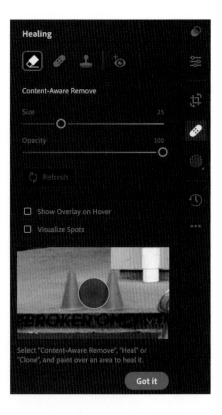

Masking

Click on the **Masking** button to access options for applying masks to elements within an image so that editing effects can be applied to a masked area without affecting the rest of the image.

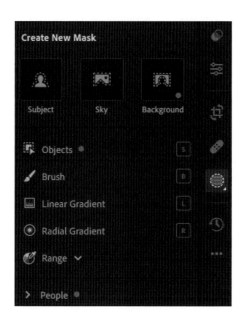

For more details about using the **Masking** and **Versions** options, see pages 126-131 and 132-136 respectively.

117

Versions

Click on the **Versions** button to create a new version of the current image once it has been edited.

Cropping

To crop an image:

1 Select an image in **Compare** view or **Detail** view, with a main subject to which you want to give more prominence

2 Click on the **Crop & Rotate** button. Cropping handles appear around the border of the image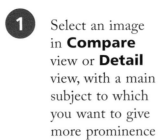

Drag the cropping handles in the middle of the horizontal and vertical borders to crop the image in these directions. Drag the corner handles to crop the image vertically and horizontally at the same time.

3 Drag the cropping handles to create an area to be included in the final image

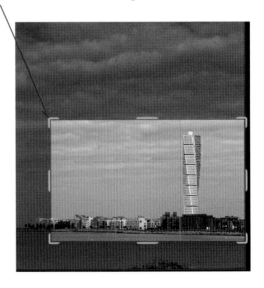

4 A cropped image should give the main subject greater prominence and significance in the image

5 Click on the **Crop Overlay** button to select the appearance of the cropping grid that is overlaid on the image when cropping is taking place

6 Different overlays can be selected depending on the image being used. This can then be used to align the final cropped image accordingly

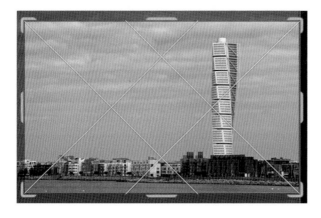

Don't forget

Click on the **Rotate & Flip** options at the bottom of the Crop panel to, from left to right: rotate the image to the left, in 90-degree increments; rotate the image to the right, in 90-degree increments; flip the image vertically; and flip the image horizontally.

Healing

The Healing option can be used to remove unwanted objects in an image. These can be large objects or smaller items such as unwanted spots in an image. There are various Healing options:

Content-Aware Remove
This is used to automatically remove a selected item and fill the area with the background around it. To do this:

Hot tip

The Content-Aware Remove function is most effective over small areas with a strong contrast between the area that you want to remove and the background.

1 Select an image in **Compare** view or **Detail** view that has an item that you want to remove. If necessary, zoom in on the image so that the area to be removed is enlarged

2 Click on the **Healing** button and click on the **Content-Aware Remove** button. Make selections as required for brush **Size** and **Opacity**

3 Drag the **Content-Aware Remove** tool over the area to be removed

Include some of the background in the selection in Step 3 so that the Content-Aware Remove tool can identify the area to be replaced, and also what it is going to be replaced with.

4 The Content-Aware Remove tool analyzes the image and displays the edited version, with the selected area removed and replaced by the background

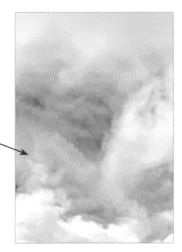

5 Check **On** the **Visualize Spots** checkbox in Step 2 on the previous page to view an image with any small random dots colored white. It may not always be necessary to remove these, but it can be done by clicking on the white dots with the Content-Aware Remove tool

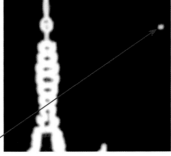

✅ Visualize Spots

...cont'd

Healing tool

The Healing tool can be used to manually select an area, and that is then healed from a sampled area. This does not copy the sampled area, but rather uses it to blend the texture, lighting, and shading with the original selection area. The sampled area can also be moved to change the appearance of the selected area.

Don't forget

The Healing tool works by selecting information from the sampled area and matching this with the selected area. This differs slightly from the Content-Aware Remove tool, which uses Artificial Intelligence (AI) to create new color information to cover the selected area.

1 Select an image with an element to be removed, perhaps because it is incongruous with the rest of the image

Don't forget

The **Feather** option in Step 2 can be used to determine the softness of the edge of a selected area so that it can be blended smoothly where it joins the rest of the image. The greater the amount of feathering – i.e. dragging the slider to the right – the softer the edges of the selection.

2 From the **Healing** options, click on the **Healing Brush** button. Make selections as required for brush **Size**, **Feather**, and **Opacity**

3 Check **On** the **Show Overlay on Hover** checkbox

4 Drag over the area of the image to be edited, which is shown as white

5 The Healing Brush tool selects an area from which the selected area will be sampled. In some cases, this will not be the required content

Hot tip

The selection and sampled areas are denoted by dotted lines if the **Show Overlay on Hover** option is checked **On** on the previous page. This arrow at the end of the dotted line denotes the direction of the sampled area toward the selected one:

123

6 Drag the sampled area to the required location so that the selected area is covered accordingly

Hot tip

Click and hold on the blue dot in the middle of the sampled area to move it as required.

...cont'd

Clone tool

The Clone tool can be used to copy items or patterns or to remove objects by copying a selected area over them. To do this:

Hot tip

Use the left bracket (**[**) key on the keyboard to decrease the size of the Clone tool before a selection is made; use the right bracket (**]**) key to increase the size.

1 Select an image with an element to be duplicated or removed

Hot tip

By default, the area selected with the Clone tool is done with a freehand selection. However, hold down the **Shift** key to create a straight line, either vertically or horizontally, for the selection area.

2 From the **Healing** options, click on the **Clone** button. Make selections as required for brush **Size**, **Feather**, and **Opacity**, and check **On** the **Show Overlay on Hover** checkbox

Hot tip

Hold down the **Ctrl** key (Windows) or the **Command** key (Mac) to select a clone area the same size as the current brush size. This is a good option for duplicating or removing small objects.

3 Drag the **Clone** tool over the area of the image to be cloned. The cloned area appears in an identically sized shape. Drag the cloned area to the appropriate point – this now covers the original selection

4 In some cases, the Clone tool can create a pattern that is visible in the image. If this is the case, use the Content-Aware Remove tool to smooth out any patterns

The cloned area moves in the direction of the arrow between the two selection areas to either hide or duplicate something.

5 To duplicate an object, swap around the selection areas in Step 3 on the previous page – i.e. so that the arrow between them is pointing from left to right

Click on this button (**Reset**) at the top of the Healing panel to remove any cloning that has been done and start again.

6 If required, the cloned item can be repositioned by dragging it around the image to create the desired effect

Masking

Masking is a sophisticated function that can be used to select specific elements of an image and apply editing effects to just the selected area. Areas can be selected manually with a variety of different tools, and selections can also be made automatically, using Lightroom's AI functionality, to select significant areas in an image, such as the sky or the main subject. To use masking:

1 Select an image to which you want to apply a masking effect; i.e. only apply editing options to a specific part of the image – in this case, the main subject

Hot tip

Use the **Objects** tool in Step 3 to make a freehand selection, or draw a rectangle around a specific object. Using AI, Lightroom will identify the object and create a mask over it. Use the **Brush** tool to draw a freehand area on an image that will serve as a mask. Use the **Linear Gradient** option to create a rectangular mask with a gradient effect. Use the **Radical Gradient** option to create an oval mask with a gradient effect.

2 Click on the **Masking** button in the right-hand toolbar

3 The masking options are displayed for creating a new mask. At the top of the panel are automated AI options. Below these are options for creating a mask manually, by drawing on the image with a selection of different tools

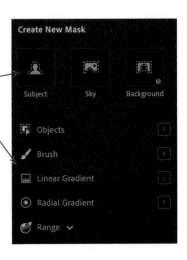

4. Click on the **Subject** option in Step 3 on the previous page to select the main subject and apply a mask over it. The mask overlay is colored red by default

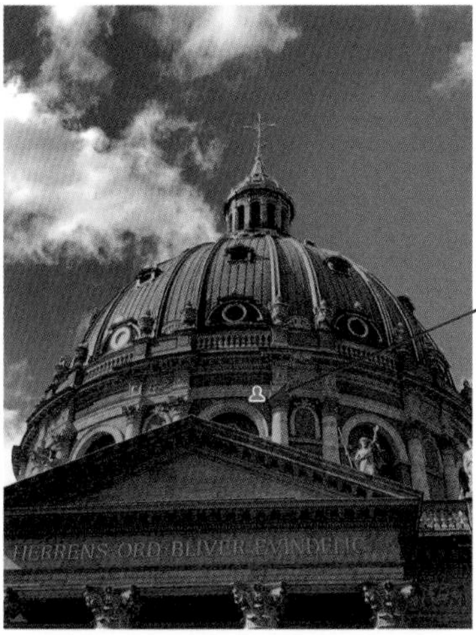

5. Zoom in on the image to ensure that the mask area has been created accurately. If not, areas can be added to – or subtracted from – the mask

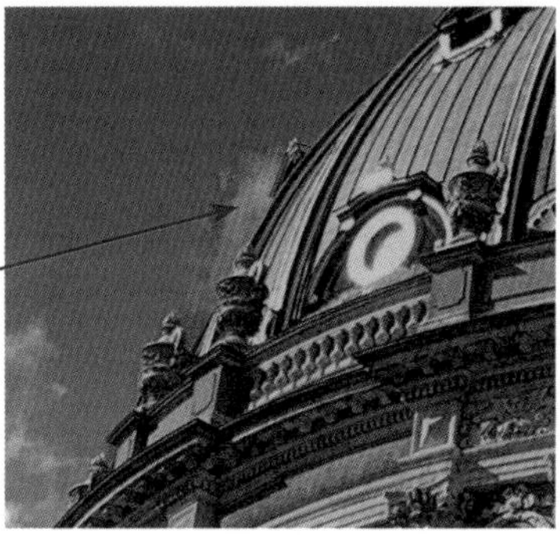

6. Click on the **Add** or **Subtract** buttons to select the required option from the Masks panel (**Subtract**, in this example)

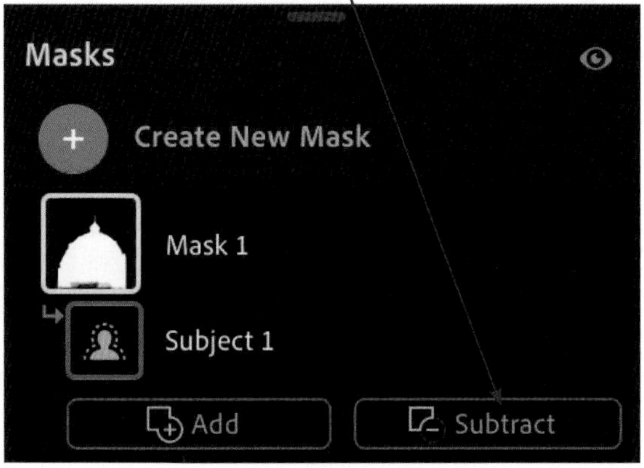

Hot tip

The red mask overlay is visible when you move the cursor over the mask area. The type of mask is denoted by a small icon on the mask – i.e. the **Subject** mask, in this example.

Don't forget

Numerous different masks can be added to a single image. Click on the **Create New Mask** option in Step 6 to add a new mask to the current image. If there are several masks linked to a single image, click on each one in the Masks panel to select it so that editing options can be applied to it. The **Add** or **Subtract** options are applied to an existing mask; they do not create a new mask.

...cont'd

7 Select a tool for drawing on the image to subtract from the mask area – e.g. **Brush**

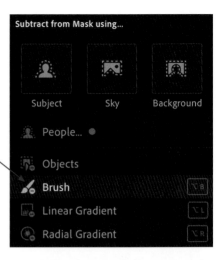

Hot tip

Reduce the brush size to add or subtract small areas in an image. The brush size can be altered several times when performing the action in Step 8.

8 Make selections for the tool selected in the previous step

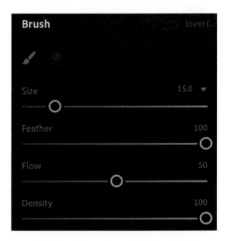

Don't forget

When an area is being added to a mask or being subtracted from it, the relevant tool icon is displayed on the image, with a − or + sign on it to denote the action being performed.

9 Drag over the area of the image to be removed from the mask (or added to it). The red mask overlay is removed from the selected area

...cont'd

10 At the top of the **Masks** panel, the original mask (**Subject 1**) is identified and also any additional masks or actions that have been added (**Brush 1**)

11 Use the editing options in the Masks panel to edit the masked object without changing anything else in the image

Drag this bar at the top of the Masks panel to the left to minimize the top section at the side of the panel so that there is more space to access the editing tools.

129

12 Click on the **Invert** option in the Masks panel to invert the selection for the mask. In this example, the subject is inverted to the sky. Apply editing to the inverted mask area – e.g. the sky – while the main subject remains unchanged

The editing options for a mask are the same as the general editing options in Lightroom.

...cont'd

Adding and removing masks

Several masks can be added to a single image, and existing masks can also be removed after they have been added.

1 To add a mask, once one has already been added to an image, click on the **Create New Mask** button in the Masks panel

2 Select a tool for creating the mask – e.g. **Objects**

3 Select an area on the image to be masked. In this example, the **Objects** tool is used to draw around an object, which is then identified automatically by the Lightroom AI function. Apply editing effects to the masked area, as required

4 The new mask is listed in the Masks panel, with the latest mask at the top of the panel

130

Beware

The order of masks cannot be changed in the **Masks** panel; the most recent mask always appears at the top of the panel. However, elements within a mask can be moved within the mask by dragging them, and they can also be moved to other masks in this way.

...cont'd

To remove a mask:

1 Move the cursor over a mask in the Masks panel. Click on the menu button that appears (three dots)

2 Click on the **Delete [ ]** button to remove the mask

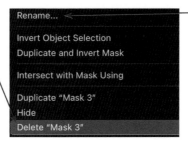

Beware

It can get confusing if you have several masks in a single image, so it is a good idea to rename them using the **Rename...** button so that each one is easy to recognize.

Managing overlays

By default, the mask overlay is colored red. The overlay can be turned **On** or **Off**, and it is also possible to change its color.

1 At the bottom of the Masks panel, drag the **Show Overlay** button **On** or **Off** to show or hide the mask overlay

2 Click on the colored circle to access the **Mask Overlay** panel for selecting a different color for the overlay

Hot tip

Click on the menu button next to the overlay color circle to access options for changing how the overlay appears.

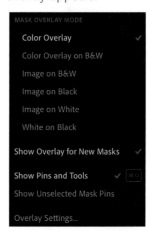

Lightroom is a non-destructive image-editing app, which means that the original image is always retained, regardless of how many editing actions are performed on it.

Versions can be saved at any time during an editing session. Several versions can be saved during a single session. The original image is always available at the bottom of the Versions panel. Click on the menu button (three dots) next to a version to access menu options, including for deleting the version.

Versions

Versions is an invaluable function in Lightroom that ensures original images are retained intact, regardless of any edits that are applied to them. In addition, all editing sessions are kept so that you can always go back to a specific point in the editing process. Versions can be created manually or automatically by Lightroom at the end of every editing session. Versions can also be used to export edited images, or the original, to other image file formats or new locations on your computer.

Named versions
To create named versions of an edited image:

1 Open the image to be edited and click on the **Versions** button in the right-hand sidebar

2 Click on the **Named** tab in the Versions panel. At this point, only the **Original** version is visible – i.e. no editing has been performed on the image

3 Perform the required edits on the image and click on the **Create Version** button

4 Enter a name for the new version and click on the **Create** button

5 An edited version is created and displayed in the **Versions** panel

...cont'd

Auto versions

To create auto versions of an edited image:

1 Open the image to be edited and click on the **Auto** tab in the Versions panel At this point, only the original version is visible – i.e. no editing has been performed on the image

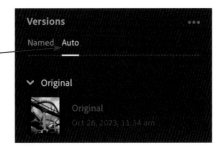

2 Perform edits on the image. The **Auto** panel remains unchanged while the editing session is taking place

3 Finish the editing session by selecting another image to make it the active one

4 Return to the original image. The editing that has been performed on it is now displayed in the **Auto** panel

5 Click on the menu button (three dots) next to a version to access its menu

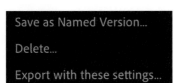

When a new **Auto** version is created, a base version is also created, denoting the starting point for where the image is edited.

The options in Step 5 are: **Save as Named Version...**, as on the previous page; **Delete...**, to remove the version but leave the original unchanged; and **Export with these settings...**, to export the image – see page 134.

133

Exporting Versions

Edited versions of an image can be exported for several reasons: to save a version in a different file format; to save a version to a different location; to save a version with a new name; or a combination of all of these. To export a new version of an image:

Don't forget

Exporting an image is, in some ways, the equivalent of saving it, since there is no Save option in Lightroom.

Don't forget

The options in Steps 1 and 2 take you directly to the window in Step 5.

134

1 In the **Versions** panel, click on the **Named** tab, then click on the menu button at the top of the panel and select one of the options for exporting an image(s)

2 For the **Auto** tab, the export options are for **All Autosaves**

3 Or, click on the **Named** or **Auto** tab and click on the menu button next to a version

4 Click on the **Export with these settings...** option

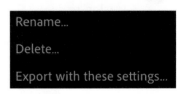

5 The **Export** window contains options for specifying settings for an exported image(s)

Do not export an image with the same filename and file format to its original location on your computer, as the exported version may overwrite the original. If you export an image to its original location, change the filename using the **File Naming** option in Step 5.

6 Select settings for elements, including **Image Type**, **Dimensions**, and **Quality**

A version of an image can be exported into multiple different file formats by repeating the processes in Steps 7 and 8.

7 Click on one of the settings to view its options – e.g. file formats from the **Image Type** option. Click on an option, as required

See page 136 for details about exporting images to a Windows computer and a Mac one.

8 Click on the **Export [ ] Photo** button

...cont'd

Exporting to Windows

To complete exporting an image to a Windows computer:

1 After you click on the **Export [ ] Photo** button in Step 8 on page 135, **File Explorer** opens. Navigate to the required folder and click on the **Select Folder** button. The image is saved in the selected folder

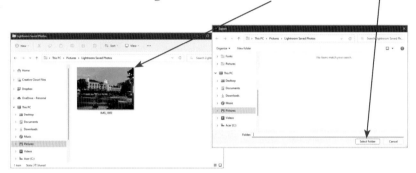

When the desktop version of Lightroom is installed, a folder named **Lightroom Saved Photos** is created automatically in the Pictures folder, for both Windows and Mac. When images are exported, this is the default folder that is selected, although it is then possible to navigate to any other folder as required.

Exporting to Mac

To complete exporting an image to a Mac computer:

1 After you click on the **Export [ ] Photo** button in Step 8 on page 135, the **Finder** opens. Navigate to the required folder and click on the **Export** button. The image is saved in the selected folder

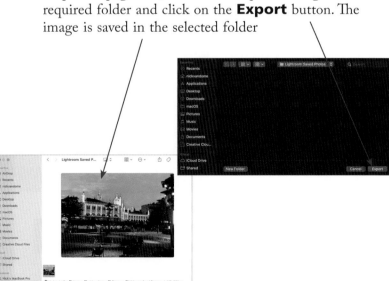

8 Mobile Lightroom

The mobile version of Lightroom, for use on smartphones and tablets, is extremely useful as it enables you to access all of your Lightroom images from wherever you are. This chapter shows how to get started with the mobile version and takes an in-depth look at its extensive features and functions.

Obtaining Mobile Lightroom

By providing a version of Lightroom for mobile devices, as well as the web and desktop versions, Adobe ensures that you can use the app to its maximum capability and capture, edit, and manage your images with any of your devices, wherever you are. The mobile version of Lightroom can be obtained from the desktop version. To do this:

138

Lightroom is free to download and use as a stand-alone app, and it can be used effectively in this way. However, if you have a Lightroom subscription, or pay for Premium Features through the app you will be able to access a wider range of editing features and cloud storage options. If you have a Lightroom subscription, the mobile version has similar features to the desktop version, and images can be shared and synced between the two.

1 Once the desktop version of Lightroom has been installed, open the Creative Cloud app, as shown on page 14, and click on the **Mobile** tab at the top of the window

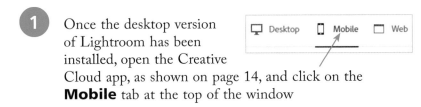

2 Click on the **Send link** button to send a link to the device on which you want to use mobile Lightroom

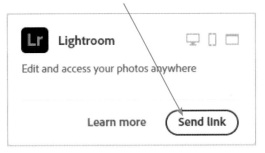

3 Select how you want the link to be sent (**SMS** text message, or **Email**) and click on the **Send Link** button

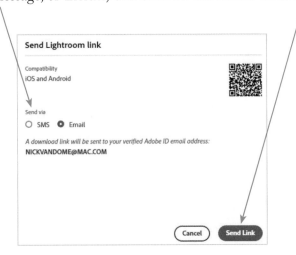

4 A message with the link is sent via the method selected in Step 3 on the previous page. Tap on the **Get Your App** button to access the mobile app

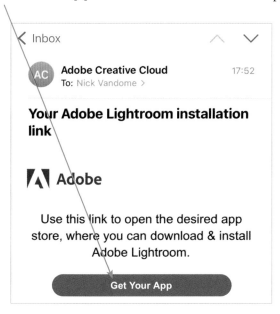

The link in Step 4 can be used to access the Lightroom app for Android smartphones and tablets, and also iPhones using iOS and iPads using iPadOS.

5 The app is available in the App Store (Apple devices) or the Google Play Store (Android devices). Tap on the **Get** button to download the app to your device

When you open the Lightroom app for the first time, you will need to sign in with your Adobe ID to access the full range of features of the app and to use it with the desktop version.

6 Access the app on your device and tap on it to open it

Mobile Interface

The mobile version of Lightroom has a more simplified interface compared with the desktop version. However, it has many of the same powerful features for accessing, editing, and sharing images. To get started with the mobile version of Lightroom:

1 Open the Lightroom app as shown on page 139. The main toolbar for navigating around the interface is located at the bottom of the screen

2 Tap on the **Lightroom** button on the bottom toolbar to view images that have been uploaded to the **Cloud** section of the desktop version of Lightroom. Any editing changes that have been made will be available in the mobile version

3 Tap on the **Device** button on the bottom toolbar

4 Images on the current device are displayed. (These are usually located in the device's Photos app.) Swipe up and down the screen to view all of these images

When viewing images in the **Device** section, some of them may already appear in the Lightroom section too, even if this is the first time that you have opened the mobile Lightroom app. This could happen if the images have been copied from your mobile device to a desktop or laptop computer and then uploaded to the **Cloud** section of the desktop version of Lightroom. Because images are synced across devices, the images will then be available in the **Lightroom** section on your mobile device.

5 Tap on the down-pointing arrowhead on **Recents** (or equivalent, depending on your device) at the top of the window in the previous step to view albums that have been created on the device, and the images within them

...cont'd

6 Tap on the **Community** button on the bottom toolbar

7 The images that are displayed are those created by members of Lightroom Community. They are displayed with presets that have been created by Community members, to give each image a unique appearance

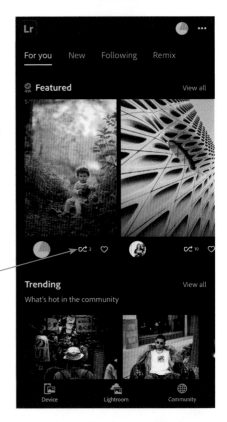

8 Tap on items on the top toolbar to view the main categories

9 For each main category, swipe on this toolbar to view the different options. Swipe up and down the screen to view the images within each category

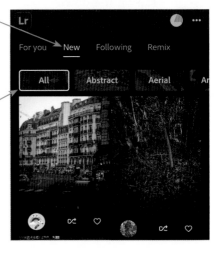

Opening Images

When opening images in the mobile version of Lightroom, the process differs slightly, depending on where you are selecting images from.

Opening Lightroom images
To open images from the **Lightroom** section:

1 Tap on the **Lightroom** button on the bottom toolbar and tap on an image to view it at full size

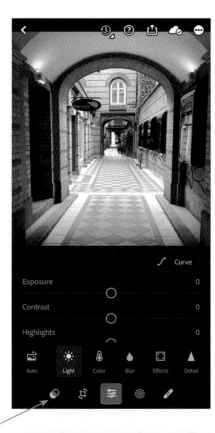

Tap on the image to view it without any of the editing tools visible. Tap on the image again to reinstate the editing tools.

2 The image opens with the editing tools automatically displayed at the bottom of the window, with the **Edit** option selected

...cont'd

Hot tip

Tap on the button at the left-hand side of the buttons shown in Step 3, and tap on the **Versions** option to

view versions of an image that have been created once editing has been applied to the image. For more information about using versions, see pages 134-136.

Hot tip

Once the **Force sync** option has been performed as in Step 2, the **Cloud** icon is displayed with green circle and a black checkmark. This indicates that it has been synced to the **Lightroom** section from the Device section. The same icon is displayed if the image is accessed at full size in the **Lightroom** section.

3 Use these buttons at the top of the window to, from left to right: create a new version of the image or reset any editing changes; access help options; save or share the image; view the cloud status of the image (synchronization); and access the menu options

4 Tap on this button (three dots) to access the menu options

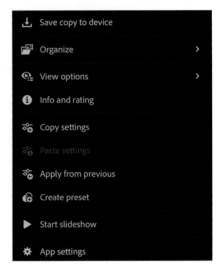

Opening Device images

Opening images from the **Device** section is similar to opening them in the **Lightroom** section, in that the editing tools are available. However, there is one important difference:

1 Tap on the Cloud icon on the top toolbar

2 Tap on the **Force sync** option to synchronize the image so that it is available in the **Lightroom** section

Opening Community images

To open images from the Community section:

1 Tap on the **Community** button on the bottom toolbar and tap on an image to view it at full size and view the preset effect that has been applied

2 Tap on the **Play edits** button at the bottom of the window

3 Editing effects that have been applied are displayed sequentially at the bottom of the window

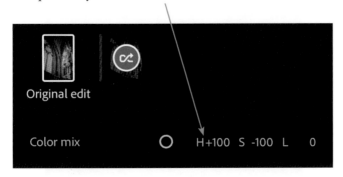

Don't forget

Use these buttons on a Community image to, from top to bottom: add your own editing effects to the original (**Remix**); save the effect; and add the effect as a favorite:

Hot tip

If there is a numbered label on the **Remix** button, this indicates the number of additional edits that have been made to it by other people.

Adding Images

The Lightroom section of the mobile app is the most effective one, as it enables full editing options while saving images in the cloud so that they can be accessed on a variety of different devices and from different locations. Therefore, it is useful to be able to add as many images as possible to the Lightroom section. For mobile devices, this can be done by adding images from the device being used and also capturing new images, which will then be available from the Lightroom section on other devices.

Adding Lightroom images
To add images to the Lightroom section from the current device being used:

Don't forget

When new images are captured by your mobile device, they are automatically available in the Lightroom Device section.

1 Tap on the **Lightroom** button on the bottom toolbar

2 When viewing images in the main **All photos** view, do not tap on an image to view it at full size, but tap on the **Add image** button in the bottom right-hand corner

Don't forget

Community images and their preset effects are updated regularly, so it is worth checking this section on a regular basis to see what is new.

3 Tap on the **Device** option to add files from the Photos app on your mobile device (other options are for adding images from another location on your device – **Files** – or from a connected digital camera or card reader)

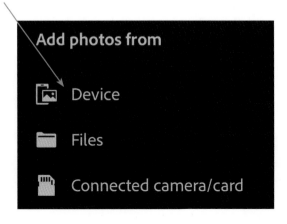

4 Tap individual images to select them, or swipe across several images to select a consecutive group

5 The number of selected images is shown at the bottom of the window. Tap on the **Add** button to add the selected images to the Lightroom section

6 The selected images are added to the Lightroom section

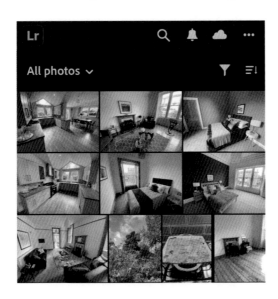

Hot tip

Tap on this button at the top right-hand side of the **All photos** window in Step 6 to select options for the order in which images appear in the window:

Hot tip

Tap on this button at the top right-hand side of the **All photos** window in Step 6 to select options for filtering which images appear in the window:

147

Color Editing

The range of editing options in the mobile version of Lightroom is similar to the ones in the desktop version. This includes comprehensive options for color editing. To use these:

 Open an image at full size in either the Lightroom or Device section and tap on the **Edit** button on the bottom toolbar

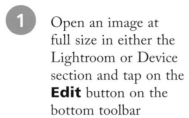

If images are edited in the Lightroom section, the edited versions will then also be available in other versions of Lightroom – e.g. the desktop and web versions.

When the **Auto** function is selected, color changes are also made in other editing categories, not just the Light one.

Tap on the **Light** button to access the relevant controls. Tap on the **Auto** button (to the left of the **Light** button) to enable Lightroom to apply automatic color edits. If **Auto** is selected, changes are displayed by the Light sliders

3 Tap on the **Curve** button at the top of the Light panel

4 Tap on the circles at the bottom of the window to select which color(s) will be edited, from left to right: all primary colors; red; green; and blue

5 Drag at points on the curved line to edit the selected color element in the image. Multiple points can be created on the curve. Tap on the **Done** button

6 Swipe up the **Light** panel to view more editing options. Drag the sliders for each option as required. As the sliders are altered, the effect is shown on the image above the sliders

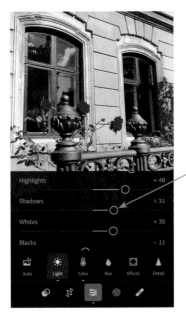

...cont'd

Swipe up the Color panel in Step 8 to access all of the options, with their sliders. These include **Temp**, **Tint**, **Vibrance**, and **Saturation**. Drag the sliders for each element, as required.

7 Tap on the **Color** button on the editing toolbar

8 The **Color** option contains similar sliders to the Light option, with additional options listed at the top of the panel

White balance refers to the process of displaying white in an image as accurately as possible so that it matches white in the real world as it was captured. If the white balance is not accurate, the image may appear with a strange color-cast effect.

9 Tap next to the **White balance** option to select how white balance in the image is selected. This determines the white point in the image and is the foundation for color editing based on this point

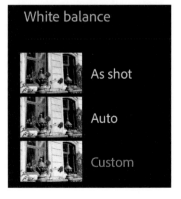

10 Tap on the white balance Eye Dropper icon in the previous step and tap on a point in the image to set this as the white point

11 Drag the **B&W** (Black & White) button at the top of the Color panel in Step 8 on the previous page **On** to convert the image to black and white

12 Tap on the **Grading** button at the top of the Color panel in Step 8 on the previous page to access options for creating a stylistic color effect. Drag on the color circles to amend the selected color effects (see the top Don't Forget tip)

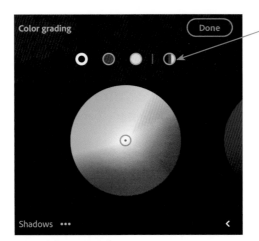

Tap on these buttons to select color grading for, from left to right: Shadows; Midtones; Highlights; and Global (all elements). For more information about using Color Grading in Lightroom, see page 99.

13 Tap on the **Color mix** button at the top of the Color panel in Step 8 to access options for amending the hue, saturation, and luminance of specific colors in the image

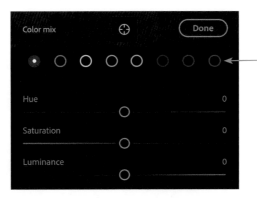

Tap on these buttons to select the required color to mix with the Color Mixer sliders. For more information about using the Color Mixer option in Lightroom, see pages 96-97.

Lens Blur

The Lens Blur feature can be used to blur areas of an image, to give the main subject more prominence. To do this:

1 Open an image in which you want to give the main subject more prominence by blurring the background or surrounding area

Beware

Ensure that there is a good contrast between the main subject and the background when using Lens Blur so that the main subject can be clearly selected.

2 Tap on the **Blur** button on the editing toolbar

3 Make selections for the type of blur effect (**Circle**, **Bubble**, **5-blade**, or **Ring**) and drag the **Blur amount** slider to apply the blur effect

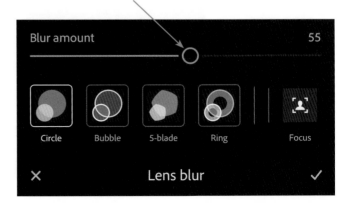

4 Tap on the **Focus** option to specify the exact area of the image to remain in focus. By default, this is **Subject**, which is identified using Artificial Intelligence (AI) by Lightroom. Tap on the **Point** option to define a specific area

Focus

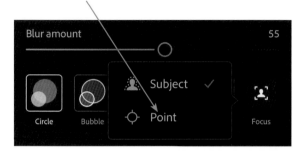

Don't forget

By default, the **Subject** option is selected for the Lens Blur function, which is identified automatically by Lightroom using AI.

5 Drag over the image to select the area to be in focus. Tap on the white checkmark in the blue circle to apply the selection area

153

6 The selected area remains in focus, with the rest of the image becoming blurred. Tap on the **Lens blur** checkmark at the bottom of the **Blur amount** panel to apply the effect, or tap on the cross to discard it

✕   Lens blur   ✓

Effects

The Effects feature can be used to apply editing effects to images that are more subtle than extreme special effects or edits.

1 Select an image to which you want to apply effects

2 Tap on the **Effects** button on the editing toolbar

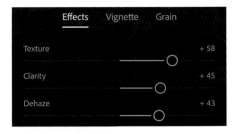

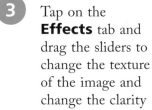

The **Dehaze** option in the Effects panel can be used to make images appear clearer if there is any mist or fog in an image.

3 Tap on the **Effects** tab and drag the sliders to change the texture of the image and change the clarity

4 Tap on the **Vignette** tab and drag the sliders to create dark or light corners around the image

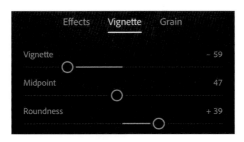

Hot tip

Drag the **Vignette** slider in Step 4 to the left to create a dark effect, or drag it to the right to create a lighter effect.

155

5 Tap on the **Grain** tab and drag the sliders to create a grainy effect similar to an impressionist painting

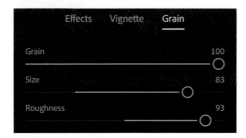

Hot tip

When the Vignette and Grain options are first accessed, there is only one slider available, for **Vignette** or **Grain** respectively. However, when this slider is moved, other options become available too.

Detail

The Detail option can be used to make images appear clearer and remove small unwanted imperfections. To use this:

1 Tap on the **Detail** button on the editing toolbar

2 Tap on the **Sharpening** tab and drag the sliders to improve the clarity of an image

3 Tap on the **Noise** tab and drag the sliders to remove small randomly appearing pixels in an image

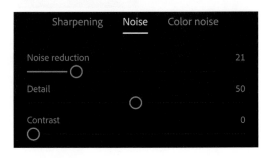

4 Tap on the **Color noise** tab and drag the sliders to remove small randomly appearing colored pixels in an image

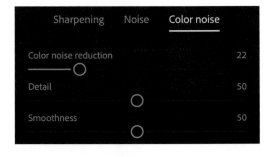

Profiles

Using profiles in the mobile version of Lightroom is similar to using them with the desktop version. They can be used to apply a collection of editing features to an image with a couple of taps. To do this in mobile Lightroom:

For more details about applying profiles, see Chapter 5.

1. Tap on the **Profiles** button on the editing toolbar

2. The **Favorites** option displays one **Color** profile and one **Monochrome** one. Tap on either of these to use them

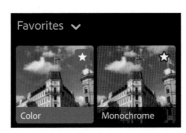

3. Tap on the **Favorites** option to view the rest of the available profiles. Tap on a category to select it

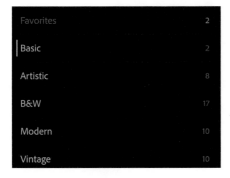

4. Tap on a profile to select it, and tap on the checkmark symbol to apply it to an image

...cont'd

5 The profile is applied to the image. Additional editing can then be applied to the image, as required

6 Different profiles can be experimented with, even after an initial profile has been applied

7 In general, profiles provide more subtle editing effects than presets – see pages 159-161

Presets

Presets are similar to profiles in that they can apply numerous editing changes in one tap. However, they can be more versatile in terms of the range of options and also because you can create your own. To use presets:

1 Select an image to which you want to apply a preset, and tap on the **Presets** button on the bottom toolbar

2 The image is displayed, with the preset options below it. Tap on the **Recommended**, **Premium**, or **Yours** options to view the main categories of presets

3 Swipe along here to view the options within each category

4 Tap on a **Recommended** preset and tap on the **More like this** option to view similar presets

5 Tap on the checkmark at the bottom of the window to apply the preset

When **Recommended** presets are first accessed for an image, Lightroom analyzes the image to ensure the most appropriate preset options are displayed.

159

Tap on this button to access a menu with a **Save to your presets** option. This then becomes available in the **Yours** category too, and you can give it a new unique name.

...cont'd

Don't forget

Presets can dramatically alter and improve images in a single tap.

6 The **Premium** presets consist of presets for specific categories – e.g. for concentrating on portraits, the sky in an image, or the main subject

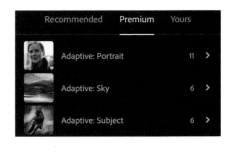

7 The **Yours** presets consist of ones that you have saved or created yourself – see below

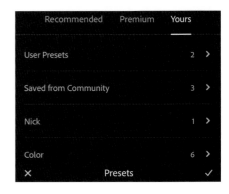

Creating presets

To create your own presets:

1 Select a preset, make editing changes to it, tap on the menu button (three dots) at the top of the window and select **Create preset**, or

2 Perform standard editing on an image, tap on the menu button at the top of the image, and select **Create preset**

3 Enter a name in the **Preset name** text box and tap on the **User Presets** option to select a location for the preset

4 Select a location for the preset. This will appear in the **Yours** section, in Step 7 on the previous page

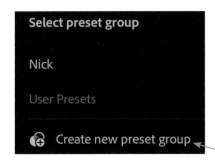

Tap on the **Create new preset group** option in Step 4 to create a customized group for saving presets. This is available in the **Yours** section of presets.

Managing presets

It is possible to hide categories of presets so that you only see the ones you use most frequently. To do this:

1 Tap on the menu button in Step 1 on the previous page and select **Manage presets**

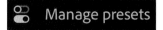 Manage presets

2 Tap on one of the available preset groups – e.g. **Premium** or **Yours**

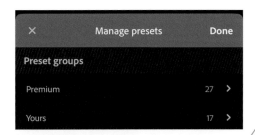

Tap on the **Done** button at the top of the **Manage presets** panel to apply any changes that have been made.

3 Drag the button next to a category to turn it **On** or **Off**. If a category is turned **Off**, it will not be available when you access that preset category

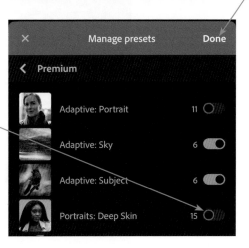

Crop & Rotate

The Crop & rotate feature can be used to emphasis a main subject by removing some unwanted background areas, and also rotating images in various ways. To crop an image:

1 Select an image to be cropped and tap on the **Crop & rotate** button on the bottom toolbar

Hot tip

Tap here to perform an automatic horizontal crop on the image, or a vertical crop if the image is in Landscape mode.

Hot tip

Tap here to select an option for a predefined ratio for the cropping tool. Tap on the **Free** button on the bottom toolbar to lock the cropping tool and constrain it to the selected aspect ratio.

Free

2 Cropping handles appear around the image

3 Drag the cropping handles to crop the image and make the main subject more prominent

Hot tip

Drag on the dial below the image to rotate it by custom amounts.

4 Tap on the checkmark on the bottom toolbar to apply cropping

Don't forget

Tap on these buttons on the bottom toolbar to, from right to left: rotate the image clockwise, in 90-degree increments; flip the image horizontally; and flip the image vertically:

5 The cropped image takes on more prominence with the background area removed

Masking

The Masking feature can be used to select specific areas of an image – e.g. the sky or a main subject – and apply editing effects to just this selected area and not the rest of the image. To do this:

Don't forget

The options for creating a mask in Step 3 include: **Select subject**, which can be used to automatically create a mask over the main subject in an image; **Select sky**, which can be used to automatically create a mask over the sky in an image; **Brush**, which can be used to make a freehand selection; **Linear gradient**, which can be used to draw a rectangular shape on an image, and a mask is then applied to the item within the selection; and **Radial gradient**, which can be used to draw an elliptical shape on an image, and a mask is then applied to the item within the selection.

1 Select an image with an area you want to edit, without altering the rest of the image, and tap on the **Masking** button on the bottom toolbar

2 Tap on this button to create a new mask

3 Select an option for the type of mask to be applied

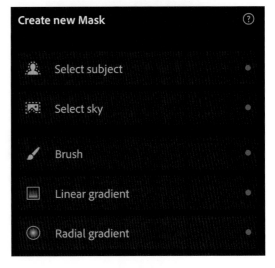

4 Tap on the **Create** button

5 A mask is created with the option selected in Step 3 on the previous page. Tap on these buttons to, from top to bottom: invert the mask – e.g. select the background; or delete the mask

A mask is denoted by a red overlay. The type of mask is denoted by an icon on the mask – e.g. a **Subject** mask.

6 Use the editing tools to perform standard editing functions on the masked area; the rest of the image remains untouched. Tap on the checkmark to apply editing effects to the mask

7 The mini masking panel is displayed in the bottom right-hand corner of the masking screen and consists of, from top to bottom: a button for adding a new mask to the image; details of the currently selected mask in the image and the type of mask used; and buttons for adding to or subtracting from the currently selected mask

Tap on an item in the mini masking panel to access its menu, if applicable. If an item has an arrowhead in the bottom right-hand corner, this indicates that there is a menu available.

Healing

The Healing feature can be used in various ways to remove unwanted areas of an image by covering them over using other parts of the image. To do this:

1 Select an image with an area you want to cover over, and tap on the **Healing** button on the bottom toolbar

The **Clone** option in Step 3 is the most effective for creating duplicates in an image, by copying one area of the image exactly to another part of the image.

2 Tap here to select options for the Healing function

3 Tap on the **Remove** option to get rid of an unwanted item in an image; tap on the **Heal** option to fill in an area based on Lightroom's AI functionality; and tap on the **Clone** option to cover an area from somewhere else in the image

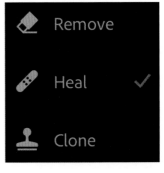

4 Drag the **Brush size** slider to select a brush size for the selected Healing option

5 Drag over the affected area of the image. The selected area is denoted by a red line as you drag on the image

> **Don't forget**
>
> For more details about working with selected and sampled areas with the Healing function, see pages 122-123.

6 For the Heal and Clone options, tap on the **Refine** button in Step 4

7 The selected and sampled areas are displayed on the image. Drag either or both of these areas around the image to get the correct combination for covering the affected area. Tap on the **Done** button when you are happy with the two areas

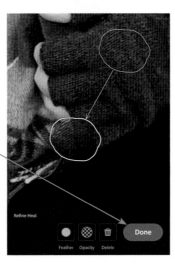

> **Hot tip**
>
> Use these buttons, at the bottom of the panel in Step 7, to, from left to right: apply a feather effect to soften the edge of a selection; set the opacity for a selection; and delete a selection:
>
>
>
> Feather   Opacity   Delete

...cont'd

8 Continue dragging over the affected area with the selected tool until the desired effect is achieved

Beware

The Healing options can be a bit hit and miss, so it can take a certain amount of time to master them and find the best ones for your own needs.

9 Tap on the checkmark to apply the Healing function that has been performed

10 Tap on the **x** symbol to discard any changes that have been made. Tap on the **Discard changes** button to confirm

9 Lightroom on the Web

The web version of Lightroom offers similar options to the desktop and mobile versions.

Accessing Web Lightroom

In addition to the desktop and mobile versions of Lightroom, there is also a web version, which is a useful option to use online if you do not have access to your own computer or mobile device.

Don't forget

The web version of Lightroom can also be accessed from a desktop computer. This is done by clicking on the **Web** tab in the Creative Cloud app and clicking on the **Launch** button next to the Lightroom app. However, there is limited value in this if you can already access Lightroom on your computing device, particularly as the web version only has the Cloud section but not the Local one.

1 Enter **lightroom.adobe.com** into a web browser and enter the sign-in details for your Adobe account (i.e. your Adobe ID, which is required to access the web version of Lightroom)

2 The web version of Lightroom launches at the **Home** section. Click on the **View all photos** button to view all of your Lightroom photos

3 Click on the **Download** button or the **Add photos** button to add more photos to Lightroom via the web version, which will be available in all other Lightroom versions

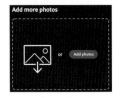

4 Scroll down the screen to view tutorials and information about using Lightroom

Web Lightroom Interface

The interface of the web version of Lightroom is similar to the desktop and mobile versions, but with some slight differences.

1 The left-hand sidebar contains the main navigation for getting around the app, including **Learn** options and Lightroom's **Community** of other users and their image edits

Click on this button in the top right-hand corner of the Home section to show or hide the sidebar.

2 Click on the **All Photos** option to view all of your Lightroom photos

3 All of the photos within Lightroom are displayed, including any edits that have been performed on images in other versions of the app

Drag this slider to change the magnification of images in the main window.

4 Click on these buttons at the left-hand side of the bottom toolbar to, from left to right: view images in an **Adaptive** grid; view images in a **Square** grid; and sort images according to various criteria

Web Color-Editing Tools

The tools for editing color and manipulating images in the web version of Lightroom are virtually the same as those for the desktop version. To use the color-editing tools:

Don't forget

For more details about using the Lightroom color-editing tools, see pages 94-99. This is for the desktop version, but using them in the web version is the same.

Beware

When viewing images at full size in the web version, there is no Filmstrip option at the bottom of the window for scrolling through images. Instead, use this option in the bottom right-hand corner to move through the available images:

< 146 of 407 >

1 Double-click on an image to view it at full size

2 Click on the **Edit** button on the right-hand toolbar. This activates the color-editing and light-editing options

3 Click on a right-pointing arrowhead to expand one of the color-editing panels and drag the sliders to apply changes, as required

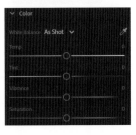

Web Presets

To use the preset options:

1 Double-click on an image to view it at full size, and click on the **Presets** button on the right-hand toolbar

For more details about using the Lightroom preset tools, see pages 60-78. This is for the desktop version, but using them in the web version is the same.

2 Click on the **Recommended**, **Premium**, and **Yours** tabs at the top of the Presets panel to access options in each of these categories

In the Recommended section, click on the buttons above the thumbnail images to view the different categories. Drag the **Amount** slider to alter the degree to which the preset is applied.

3 Click on a preset to apply it to the current image

Web Manipulation Tools

As with the color-editing tools, the tools for manipulating images in the web version of Lightroom are very similar to the desktop version.

Crop & Rotate

To use the Crop & Rotate tools:

1 Click on the **Crop & Rotate** button on the right-hand toolbar

2 Select an option for cropping the image and drag around the area you want to keep. Use the **Rotate & Flip** options to change the rotation of the image, and the **Geometry** options to change the perspective

Healing

To use the Healing tools:

1 Click on the **Healing** button on the right-hand toolbar

2 Select the **Content-Aware Remove** tool and make selections for it, as required

For more details about using the Lightroom Crop & Rotate tools, see pages 118-119. For the Geometry tools, see pages 110-114. These are for the desktop version, but using them in the web version is the same.

For more details about using the Lightroom Healing tools, see pages 120-125. This is for the desktop version, but using them in the web version is the same.

Don't forget

Don't forget

3 Select the **Heal** tool and make selections for it, as required

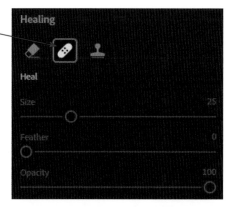

4 Select the **Clone** tool and make selections for it, as required

Masking
To use the Masking tools:

1 Click on the **Masking** button on the right-hand toolbar

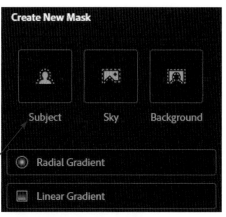

2 Select one of the masking options – e.g. **Subject**, **Sky**, or **Background** – to have it applied automatically

For more details about using the Lightroom Masking tools, see pages 126-131. This is for the desktop version, but using them in the web version is the same.

Other masking options, such as **Radial Gradient** and **Linear Gradient**, can be applied manually by dragging on an image to select an area to which the mask is applied.

...cont'd

Versions

To use the Versions tools:

For more details about using the Lightroom Versions tools, see pages 132-136. This is for the desktop version, but using them in the web version is the same.

Don't forget

1 Click on the **Versions** button on the right-hand toolbar

2 Click on the **Auto** tab at the top of the **Versions** panel. This creates a new version when editing changes have been applied, and then another image is accessed. When you return to the edited image, a new version will be displayed in the Auto section

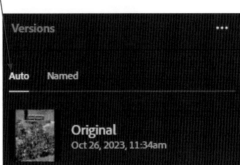

Hot tip

Click on the menu button (three dots) at the bottom of the toolbar at the right-hand side of the Lightroom window to access options for resetting an image that has had editing changes applied to it. This can be used for any editing changes.

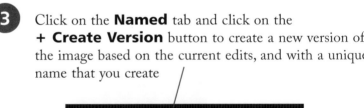

3 Click on the **Named** tab and click on the **+ Create Version** button to create a new version of the image based on the current edits, and with a unique name that you create

176

10 Searching and Organizing

This chapter shows how to tag and search for images, and also how to create albums and share them.

Tagging and Keywords

Lightroom can be used to view, manage, and edit thousands of images. However, this can mean that, after a time, it can be hard to locate the exact images that you want. But there are several options to make searching for images easier, including tags and keywords.

Hot tip

The **Add a keyword** option can also be selected from the **Photo** menu in Step 1. There is also an **Edit Date & Time...** option for when an image was captured – for instance, if you are in another country and have not reset the date and time on your camera.

Add a keyword
Edit Date & Time...

1 In the desktop version of Lightroom, select an image in either **Compare** view or **Detail** view and click on the **Photo** menu on the top menu bar

Photo View Help	
Set Rating:	
None	0
1 Star	1
2 Stars	2
3 Stars	3
4 Stars	4
5 Stars	5
Set Flag:	
Unflagged	U
Pick	Z
Reject	X
Increase Flag Status	Ctrl+Up
Decrease Flag Status	Ctrl+Down
Add to Album	>
Add a keyword	Ctrl+K
Edit Date & Time...	

2 Select the **Set Rating:** or **Set Flag:** options to tag the image in this way

3 Click on the **Keywords** button in the bottom right-hand corner of the Lightroom window to access the option for adding keywords to an image

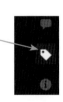

4 Use the **Keywords** text box to add a keyword to the currently selected image

Keywords

Add a keyword

5 Enter the required keyword into the text box and press the **Enter** key on the keyboard

6 Whenever the image is selected, any keywords that have been added are shown in the **Keywords** panel, below the Keywords text box

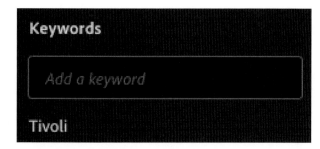

7 To add a keyword to multiple images at the same time, access **Photo Grid** or **Square Grid** view. Select images as required, and enter a keyword as above. This will be applied to all selected images

Don't forget

To select multiple consecutive images, click on the first image, hold down the **Shift** key, and click on the last image in the sequence. To select multiple non-consecutive images, click on the first image, hold down the **Ctrl** key (Windows) or **Command** key (Mac), and click on more images as required.

179

Hot tip

If a keyword has already been added to a single image, this will appear as a suggestion when you want to apply keywords to multiple images. Click on the suggestion to apply that keyword to selected images.

Searching

The Search facility in Lightroom is a powerful one: it can be used to search for images to which tags and keywords have been applied, and it can also search over a variety of criteria based on metadata that is captured by the camera at the time that the image is taken. To search for images in desktop Lightroom:

Don't forget

To search for items using the mobile version of Lightroom, tap on the Search icon at the top of the window to access the Search box.

Enter a keyword or search category into the Search box. Matching results are shown in the main window.

1 Click in the **Search All Photos** text box, which is available at the top of the Lightroom window in all views

2 A range of categories for searching is displayed, including those for **Camera Settings**, **Metadata**, and **File** details. Click on a category, as required

Don't forget

If any ratings or flag tags have been added, as in Step 2 on page 178, these can be used for searching for images too.

3 For the item selected in Step 2, sub-categories are listed in the Search panel. Click on items as required to include or exclude them in the search. Press the **Enter** button. Matching search items are shown in the main window

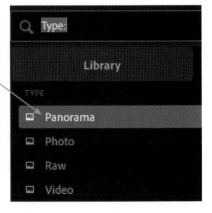

Searching with keywords

In addition to searching using the items on the previous page, images can also be searched for using keywords that have been added to them. To do this:

1 Type the required keyword into the **Search All Photos** window and press the **Enter** button. All images with the matching keyword are displayed in the main window

2 Searches can be refined with keywords by adding multiple keywords to images. Once this has been done, add two or more keywords in the Search box to refine the search to only images with both/all keywords

Hot tip

To remove a keyword from an image, move the cursor over it in the Keywords panel until it turns red with a line through it. Click on the highlighted keyword to remove it.

Beware

Enter a semi-colon (;) between multiple keyword searches to get the most accurate result.

Albums

Images in Lightroom can be organized into individual albums to make it easier to find items according to subject matter. To create albums and add images to them:

Don't forget

Lightroom Team Photos is an album that is pre-inserted when Lightroom is first installed.

Don't forget

Click on this option in the top right-hand corner of the Albums section to access a menu for sorting and viewing included albums.

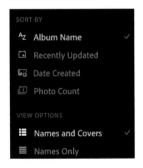

1 The **Albums** section is located in the left-hand sidebar of the Lightroom interface

2 Click on the **+** button and click on the **Create Album...** button

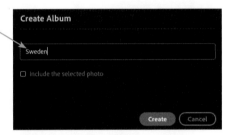

3 Enter a name for the new album and click on the **Create** button

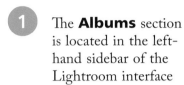

4 The newly created album is available in the **Albums** section

5 In the main window is an **Add Photos** option. This is done from File Manager (Windows) or Finder (Mac) and is used for images that are not already in Lightroom

Adding images to an album

To add existing Lightroom images to an album:

1 Right-click on an image, or images

2 Click on **Add [ ] Photo(s) to Album**

Albums are not available in the **Local** view of desktop Lightroom.

3 Click on the required album, or

4 Select an image, or images, in **Photo Grid** or **Square Grid** view

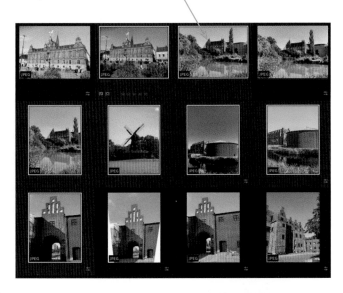

Selected images have a white border around them to identify that they have been selected. The right-click option in Steps 1-3 can also be used if multiple images are selected.

5 Drag the selected image(s) over the album name in the **Albums** section in the sidebar

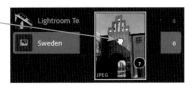

...cont'd

Don't forget

Images in albums are not physically stored in their albums; the album entry is a reference to where the image is located within Lightroom. Album images can be accessed in all Lightroom views.

Beware

Images can be deleted from albums by right-clicking on them and clicking on the **Remove [ ] Photo from Album** option. This only removes the image from an album, not its location in Lightroom. However, if you right-click on an image, there is also a **Delete [ ] Photo** option, which does remove the image from Lightroom.

6 The number of images in each album is denoted to the right of the album name

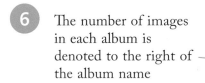

7 Click on an album name to view the images within it

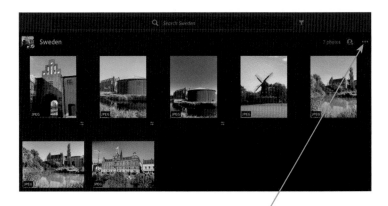

8 Click on the menu button (three dots) in the top right-hand corner of an album

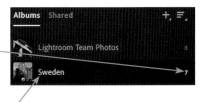

9 Select options accessed above, including sharing an album with **Share & Invite...**, renaming an album, and deleting an album

Share & Invite...

Rename Album

Delete Album "Sweden"...

Set "Sweden" as the Target Album

Make Album Available Offline

10 Right-click on an album name in the Albums panel to access a similar menu to the one in Step 9 for the album

Share To   >
Share & Invite...

Rename Album...

Set "Sweden" as the Target Album
Make Album Available Offline

Delete Album...

Sharing Images

The sharing options in Lightroom can be used to share images with family and friends, share them with other people in Lightroom Community, or export them into different formats. To use the sharing options:

1 Access an image in **Detail** view or **Compare** view, or select one or more in **Photo Grid** or **Square Grid** view

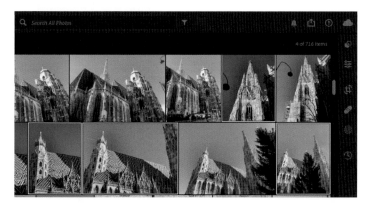

When images are selected in either Photo Grid view or Square Grid view, this is indicated by a white border around them.

2 Click on the **Share** button on the top toolbar

3 Click on one of the **Share** options – either **Get a Link...** or **Invite People...**, both of which open the same window

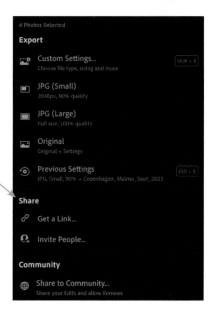

The Share panel also has options for exporting images into other file formats, as shown on pages 28-29. There is also an option for sharing images using Lightroom Community. See pages 24-27 for more details about Lightroom Community.

...cont'd

④ If the **Invite People...** option is selected in Step 3 on page 185, click on the **Get shareable link...** button. (If the **Get a Link...** option is selected in Step 3 on page 185, the link will already be inserted here)

Beware

The **Invite only** option in Step 6 is the most secure one in terms of allowing people to view your Lightroom images.

⑤ A link for sharing the image is inserted into the text box

⑥ Click here to select who can view the linked image

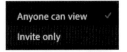

⑦ Enter an email address(es) for anyone you want to view the image using the inserted link, and click on the **Invite** button. The recipient(s) will receive an email containing the link, from which the image can be accessed

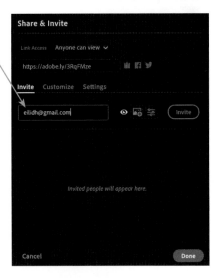

⑧ Click on the **Done** button

Index

W

Y

Z